AS IT IS WRITTEN:
KINGDOM OF GOD;
The Ultimate Kingdom

CLAUDETTE GUNTER

AS IT IS WRITTEN: KINGDOM OF GOD

Copyright © 2017 by Claudette Gunter
7600 W. Roosevelt Rd
Lower Level, Suite 11
Forest Park, IL 60130

First Edition. All rights reserved.
Published in the United States of America.

All Scripture quotations in Giving Is God is taken from the King James Version of the Bible, unless otherwise noted are the following:

Scripture quotations marked (KJV) are taken from the Holy Bible, King James Version, Cambridge, 1769. Used by permission. All rights reserved.

Scripture quotations marked (AMPC®) are taken from the Amplified Bible, Classic Edition ® Copyright © 1954, 1958, 1962, 1964, 1965, 1987 by The Lockman Foundation. Used by permission

Scripture taken from the New King James Version® (NKJV®), Copyright © 1982 by Thomas Nelson. Used by permission. All rights reserved.

Scripture quotations marked (MSG) are taken from The Message. Copyright © 1993, 1994, 1995, 1996, 2000, 2001, 2002. Used by permission of NavPress Publishing Group.

Scripture quotations taken from the New American Standard Bible® (NASB), Copyright © 1960, 1962, 1963, 1968, 1971, 1972, 1973, 1975, 1977, 1995 by The Lockman Foundation Used by permission. www.Lockman.org

As it is written from the Word of God
Published by Claudette Gunter
Thoughts expressed by author. All rights reserved.
Author's website at www.kingdomofGodflag.com/®.

Cover design by author

No part of this publication may be reproduced, stored in a retrieval system or transmitted in any way by any means, electronic, mechanical, photocopy, recording or otherwise without the prior permission of the author except as provided by USA copyright law.

ISBN: 978-0-9990833-5-2

AS IT IS WRITTEN:

KINGDOM OF GOD;
The Ultimate Kingdom

✝ "And the seventh angel sounded; and there were great voices in Heaven, saying, The kingdoms of this world are become the kingdoms of our Lord, and of His Christ; and He shall reign for ever and ever. **Revelation 11:15**"

ACKNOWLEDGMENT

I definitely have to acknowledge You; my Father God, because I know nothing is possible without You (**Mark 10:27**). I know that I can not do anything without Christ (**Philippians 4:13**), so I Thank You, my Lord Jesus for Your Precious Blood. I especially know that if I could not hear You; my Holy Spirit (**Romans 8:14**), this book would not have been thought of. Thank You Holy Ghost for bringing God's Word to my remembrance. I give to You, my God; Holy Trinity all the honor, glory and praise. Thank You for loving me first, so that I can know Who Love is (**1 John 4**), and how to love You back. Now I can share Your love with others !!!

† **Proverbs 3:5-6 (AMPC)** Lean on, trust in, and be confident in the Lord with all your heart and mind and do not rely on your own insight or understanding. In all your ways know, recognize, and acknowledge Him, and He will direct and make straight and plain your paths.

† **Mark 10:27 (KJV)** And Jesus looking upon them saith, With men it is impossible, but not with God: for with God all things are possible.

† **John 5:19 (KJV)** Then answered Jesus and said unto them, Verily, verily, I say unto you, The Son can do

nothing of himself, but what he seeth the Father do: for what things soever he doeth, these also doeth the Son likewise.

† **John 5:30 (AMPC)** I am able to do nothing from Myself [independently, of My own accord—but only as I am taught by God and as I get His orders]. Even as I hear, I judge [I decide as I am bidden to decide. As the voice comes to Me, so I give a decision], and My judgment is right (just, righteous), because I do not seek or consult My own will [I have no desire to do what is pleasing to Myself, My own aim, My own purpose] but only the will and pleasure of the Father Who sent Me.

† **John 15:4-6 (NKJV)** Abide in Me, and I in you. As the branch cannot bear fruit of itself, unless it abides in the vine, neither can you, unless you abide in Me. "I am the vine, you are the branches. He who abides in Me, and I in him, bears much fruit; for without Me you can do nothing. If anyone does not abide in Me, he is cast out as a branch and is withered; and they gather them and throw them into the fire, and they are burned.

† **Romans 8:14 (KJV)** For as many as are led by the Spirit of God, they are the sons of God.

† **2 Corinthians 13:8 (AMPC)** For we can do nothing against the Truth [not serve any party or personal interest], but only for the Truth [which is the Gospel].

† **Philippians 4:13 (KJV)** I can do all things through Christ which strengtheneth me.

† **1 Peter 1:6-8 (NLV)** 6. With this hope you can be happy even if you need to have sorrow and all kinds of tests for awhile. 7. These tests have come to prove your faith and to show that it is good. Gold, which can be destroyed, is tested by fire. Your faith is worth much more than gold and it must be tested also. Then your faith will bring thanks and shining-greatness and honor to Jesus Christ when He comes again. 8. You have never seen Him but you love Him. You cannot see Him now but you are putting your trust in Him. And you have joy so great that words cannot tell about it.

† **1 John 4:7-9 (KJV)** Beloved, let us love one another: for love is of God; and every one that loveth is born of God, and knoweth God. He that loveth not knoweth not God; for God is love. In this was manifested the love of God toward us, because that God sent his only begotten Son into the world, that we might live through him.

† **1 John 4:19 (KJV)** We love him, because he first loved us.

CONTENTS

	Introduction	xi
1	Kingdom of God	1
2	Father God	7
3	Jesus Christ	15
4	Holy Spirit	25
5	Holy Bible	31
6	Who WE are?	39
7	Why are WE here?	53
	About the Author	101

INTRODUCTION

The reason for this title "AS IT IS WRITTEN ..., it is declaring what to expect throughout this book; the WORD OF GOD !!! God's word is so good, that I came to the conclusion (duh), why try to explain Jesus, when His Word speaks for Himself, plus He has His Spirit to bring His Word alive with power (**as we give voice to His Word – that's the key for its wonderful working power to manifest in our lives: "We have to speak His words"**).

So, after praying about what He would have me to do next, I listened. All I had to do here was put in some titles and give a paragraph or so. I really enjoy God's Word. All I rather do is hear and read His Word. You know what I mean if you enjoy His Word like me. Oh yes and take action. Action is applying what the Holy Spirit reveals to us through His Word and/or to our spirit concerning our everyday life. Enjoy !!!

This book is to reveal through scripture, our King; Jesus, the Kingdom of God; our Government (Thee Holy Trinity) and who we are as the Church and why we are here.

<u>Disclaimer & Disclosure</u>: Be free to search the Bible for yourselves, for I am not a bible scholar, but I am a son of God. I know I can't get all of God's Word in this book, if so what would be the use for this book, when we all can go directly to our own Bibles. My hope is to release a desire in you to search the scriptures, so that the Holy Spirit can teach you about the things that you seek. ~ Claudette

KINGDOM OF GOD
Our Government
(Our country & home is Heaven)

The Kingdom of God is the government of Heaven. This is the government that was announced in Isaiah 9. It is a kingdom of power and authority that governs with justice and peace. The Kingdom of God is within me and you when we are saved; born again.

We, the citizens of the Kingdom of Heaven, must enforce justice on earth as it is in Heaven. In all that we do, we must seek first God's Kingdom and His righteousness. Our Lord and King Jesus and His Kingdom reigns over all and shall reign forever and ever, Amen !!!

Definition of a kingdom: n. [king and dom, jurisdiction.] The territory or country subject to a king; an undivided territory under the dominion of a king or monarch.

In Scripture, the government and dominion of God:

† **Deuteronomy 26:15 (AMPC)** Look down from Your holy habitation, from heaven, and bless Your people Israel and the land which You have given us as You swore to our fathers, a land flowing with milk and honey.

† **1 Chronicles 29:11-13 (KJV)** 11. Thine, O Lord is the greatness, and the power, and the glory, and the victory, and the majesty: for all that is in the heaven and in the earth is thine; thine is the kingdom, O Lord, and thou art exalted as head above all. 12. Both riches and honour come of thee, and thou reignest over all; and in thine hand is power and might; and in thine hand it is to make great, and to give strength unto all. 13. Now therefore, our God, we thank thee, and praise thy glorious name.

† **Psalm 22:28 (AMPC)** For the kingship and the kingdom are the Lord's, and He is the ruler over the nations.

† **Psalm 103:18-20 (AMPC)** 18. To such as keep His covenant [hearing, receiving, loving, and obeying it] and to those who [earnestly] remember His commandments to do them [imprinting them on their hearts]. 19. The Lord has established His throne in the heavens, and His kingdom rules over all. 20. Bless (affectionately, gratefully praise) the Lord, you His angels, you mighty ones who do His commandments, hearkening to the voice of His word.

† **Isaiah 9:7 (AMPC)** Of the increase of His government and of peace there shall be no end, upon the throne of David and over his kingdom, to establish it and to uphold it with justice and with righteousness

from the [latter] time forth, even forevermore. The zeal of the Lord of hosts will perform this.

† **Matthew 3:2 (AMP)** "Repent [change your inner self—your old way of thinking, regret past sins, live your life in a way that proves repentance; seek God's purpose for your life], for the kingdom of heaven is at hand."

† **Matthew 6:10 (KJV)** Thy kingdom come, Thy will be done in earth, as it is in heaven.

† **Matthew 6:33 (KJV)** But seek ye first the kingdom of God, and his righteousness; and all these things shall be added unto you.

† **Matthew 13:47-48 (KJV)** Again, the kingdom of heaven is like unto a net, that was cast into the sea, and gathered of every kind: Which, when it was full, they drew to shore, and sat down, and gathered the good into vessels, but cast the bad away.

† **Mark 4:26–28 (AMPC)** And He said, The kingdom of God is like a man who scatters seed upon the ground, And then continues sleeping and rising night and day while the seed sprouts and grows and increases—he knows not how. The earth produces [acting] by itself—first the blade, then the ear, then the full grain in the ear.

† **Luke 8:10 (AMPC)** He said to them, To you it has been given to [come progressively to] know (to recognize and understand more strongly and clearly) the mysteries and secrets of the kingdom of God, but for others they are in parables, so that, [though] looking, they may not see; and hearing, they may not comprehend.

† **Luke 13:18–19 (NASB)** So He was saying, "What is the kingdom of God like, and to what shall I compare it? It is like a mustard seed, which a man took and threw into his own garden; and it grew and became a tree, and THE BIRDS OF THE AIR NESTED IN ITS BRANCHES."

† **Luke 17:20–21 (NASB)** Now having been questioned by the Pharisees as to when the kingdom of God was coming, He answered them and said, "The kingdom of God is not coming with signs to be observed; nor will they say, 'Look, here it is!' or, 'There it is!' For behold, the kingdom of God is in your midst."

† **John 3:5 (NASB)** Jesus answered, "Truly, truly, I say to you, unless one is born of water and the Spirit he cannot enter into the kingdom of God.

† **John 18:33-38 (AMPC)** 33. So Pilate went back again into the judgment hall and called Jesus and asked Him, Are You the King of the Jews? 34. Jesus replied, Are you saying this of yourself [on your own initiative], or

have others told you about Me? 35. Pilate answered, Am I a Jew? Your [own] people *and* nation and their chief priests have delivered You to me. What have You done? 36. Jesus answered, My kingdom (kingship, royal power) belongs not to this world. If My kingdom were of this world, My followers would have been fighting to keep Me from being handed over to the Jews. But as it is, My kingdom is not from here (this world); [it has no such origin or source]. 37. Pilate said to Him, Then You are a King? Jesus answered, You say it! [You speak correctly!] For I am a King. [Certainly I am a King!] This is why I was born, and for this I have come into the world, to bear witness to the Truth. Everyone who is of the Truth [who is a friend of the Truth, who belongs to the Truth] hears *and* listens to My voice. 38. Pilate said to Him, What is Truth? On saying this he went out to the Jews again and told them, I find no fault in Him.

† **Acts 1:3 (AMPC)** To them also He showed Himself alive after His passion (His suffering in the garden and on the cross) by [a series of] many convincing demonstrations [unquestionable evidences and infallible proofs], appearing to them during forty days and talking [to them] about the things of the kingdom of God.

† **Acts 14:22 (NASB)** Confirming the souls of the disciples, and exhorting them to continue in the faith,

and that we must through much tribulation enter into the kingdom of God.

† **Acts 28:31 (KJV)** Preaching the kingdom of God, and teaching those things which concern the Lord Jesus Christ, with all confidence, no man forbidding him.

† **Acts 28:31 (CEV)** He bravely preached about God's kingdom and taught about the Lord Jesus Christ, and no one tried to stop him.

† **Philippians 3:20 (AMPC)** But we are citizens of the state (commonwealth, homeland) which is in heaven, and from it also we earnestly and patiently await [the coming of] the Lord Jesus Christ (the Messiah) [as] Savior,

† **Hebrews 12:28 (NKJV)** Therefore, since we are receiving a kingdom which cannot be shaken, let us have grace, by which we may serve God acceptably with reverence and godly fear.

† **Revelation 11:15 (KJV)** And the seventh angel sounded; and there were great voices in Heaven, saying, The kingdoms of this world are become the kingdoms of our Lord, and of His Christ; and He shall reign for ever and ever.

FATHER GOD: Our Father

Father God is our Creator and He is Spirit, He is our Source of life and I am so honored that He chose me. I acknowledge He is real. He is more real than anyone who doubts His existence.

Doubting? Believe it or not, we have control over our situation and circumstance, by the decisions we make. Things may not happen all at once, whether consequences or by His favor, but you will sense that something is happening. I personally can see God working in my life and what concerns me. The more we focus on the Word of God, the more we are transforming to His image and likeness in the way that He planned it, before the foundation of the world.

By the renewing of our mind with the Word of God, we will start thinking like Jesus. Our faith will continuously grow and we will have the manifestation in our lives, we desire. Yes, we may miss Him sometimes, but when we see what we are doing is not pleasing to God, don't run from God, run to Him for His help. Ask for forgiveness and He will forgive us and restore us, besides where can we hide from God? He is Omnipresent. Remember, He is our Creator, He can and will fix us, if we let Him. He loves us unconditionally.

Father God has many names for His many attributes. God is Three Persons in One: Trinity; God the Father, God the Son-Jesus and God the Holy Spirit. Father God is the #1

Love of the Trinity, which is the reason we exist. I invite you to get to know Him or even better through His Word, you will never regret being in His Presence.

† **Genesis 1:1-4 (KJV)** In the beginning God created the heaven and the earth. And the earth was without form, and void; and darkness was upon the face of the deep. And the Spirit of God moved upon the face of the waters. And God said, Let there be light: and there was light. And God saw the light, that it was good: and God divided the light from the darkness.

† **Genesis 1:26-27 (KJV)** And God said, Let us make man in our image, after our likeness: and let them have dominion over the fish of the sea, and over the fowl of the air, and over the cattle, and over all the earth, and over every creeping thing that creepeth upon the earth. So God created man in his own image, in the image of God created he him; male and female created he them.

† **Exodus 3:14 (KJV)** And God said unto Moses, I Am That I Am: and he said, Thus shalt thou say unto the children of Israel, I Am hath sent me unto you.

† **Deuteronomy 7:9 (KJV)** Know therefore that the Lord thy God, he is God, the faithful God, which keepeth covenant and mercy with them that love him and keep his commandments to a thousand generations;

☦ **Psalm 2:4 (AMPC)** He Who sits in the heavens laughs; the Lord has them in derision [and in supreme contempt He mocks them].

☦ **Psalm 115:16 (KJV)** The heaven, even the heavens, are the Lord's: but the earth hath he given to the children of men.

☦ **Matthew 6:9-15 (KJV)** 9. After this manner therefore pray ye: Our Father which art in heaven, Hallowed be thy name. 10. Thy kingdom come, Thy will be done in earth, as it is in heaven. 11. Give us this day our daily bread. 12. And forgive us our debts, as we forgive our debtors. 13. And lead us not into temptation, but deliver us from evil: For thine is the kingdom, and the power, and the glory, for ever. Amen. 14. For if ye forgive men their trespasses, your heavenly Father will also forgive you: 15. But if ye forgive not men their trespasses, neither will your Father forgive your trespasses.

☦ **Matthew 6:33 (AMPC)** But seek (aim at and strive after) first of all His kingdom and His righteousness (His way of doing and being right), and then all these things taken together will be given you besides.

☦ **John 1:29 (KJV)** The next day John seeth Jesus coming unto him, and saith, Behold the Lamb of God, which taketh away the sin of the world.

† **John 3:16 (KJV)** For God so loved the world, that he gave his only begotten Son, that whosoever believeth in him should not perish, but have everlasting life.

† **John 3:16-17 (NKJV)** For God so loved the world that He gave His only begotten Son, that whoever believes in Him should not perish but have everlasting life. For God did not send His Son into the world to condemn the world, but that the world through Him might be saved.

† **John 4:23-24 (AMPC)** A time will come, however, indeed it is already here, when the true (genuine) worshipers will worship the Father in spirit and in truth (reality); for the Father is seeking just such people as these as His worshipers. God is a Spirit (a spiritual Being) and those who worship Him must worship Him in spirit and in truth (reality).

† **John 14:10 (AMPC)** Do you not believe that I am in the Father, and that the Father is in Me? What I am telling you I do not say on My own authority *and* of My own accord; but the Father Who lives continually in Me does the (*His*) works (His own miracles, deeds of power).

† **John 16:23 (KJV)** And in that day ye shall ask me nothing. Verily, verily, I say unto you, Whatsoever ye shall ask the Father in my name, he will give it you.

† **Acts 7:48-50 (KJV)** Howbeit the most High dwelleth not in temples made with hands; as saith the prophet, Heaven is my throne, and earth is my footstool: what house will ye build me? saith the Lord: or what is the place of my rest? Hath not my hand made all these things?

† **Romans 3:3-4 (KJV)** For what if some did not believe? shall their unbelief make the faith of God without effect? God forbid: yea, let God be true, but every man a liar; as it is written, That thou mightest be justified in thy sayings, and mightest overcome when thou art judged.

† **Romans 8:14-16 (AMPC)** For all who are led by the Spirit of God are sons of God. For [the Spirit which] you have now received [is] not a spirit of slavery to put you once more in bondage to fear, but you have received the Spirit of adoption [the Spirit producing sonship] in [the bliss of] which we cry, Abba (Father)! Father! The Spirit Himself [thus] testifies together with our own spirit, [assuring us] that we are children of God.

† **1 Corinthians 1:9 (AMPC)** God is faithful (reliable, trustworthy, and therefore ever true to His promise, and He can be depended on); by Him you were called into companionship and participation with His Son, Jesus Christ our Lord.

✝ **Galatians 4:5-7 (NKJV)** ... to redeem those who were under the law, that we might receive the adoption as sons. And because you are sons, God has sent forth the Spirit of His Son into your hearts, crying out, "Abba, Father!" Therefore you are no longer a slave but a son, and if a son, then an heir of God through Christ.

✝ **1 John 1:9 (KJV)** If we confess our sins, he is faithful and just to forgive us our sins, and to cleanse us from all unrighteousness.

✝ **John 4:24 (KJV)** God is a Spirit: and they that worship him must worship him in spirit and in truth.

✝ **1 John 4:7-8 (KJV)** Beloved, let us love one another: for love is of God; and every one hat loveth is born of God, and knoweth God. He that loveth not knoweth not God; for God is love.

✝ **Colossians 1:12-14 (KJV)** 12. Giving thanks unto the Father, which hath made us meet to be partakers of the inheritance of the saints in light: 13. Who hath delivered us from the power of darkness, and hath translated us into the kingdom of his dear Son: 14. In whom we have redemption through his blood, even the forgiveness of sins:

✝ **Colossians 1:12-17 (NKJV)** Giving thanks to the Father who has qualified us to be partakers of the inheritance of the saints in the light. He has delivered us from the power of darkness and conveyed us into the kingdom of the Son of His love, in whom we have redemption through His blood, the forgiveness of sins. He is the image of the invisible God, the firstborn over all creation. For by Him all things were created that are in heaven and that are on earth, visible and invisible, whether thrones or dominions or principalities or powers. All things were created through Him and for Him. And He is before all things, and in Him all things consist.

CLAUDETTE GUNTER

JESUS CHRIST: Our King

Jesus Christ is my Lord and Savior and my King. He is the Son of God, the Messiah, Anointed One, our Redeemer, Healer, Elder Brother and the Word. Jesus is the 2nd Person in the Trinity. Though He is God in the flesh; He is the Voice of God, the written Word. If not for Jesus, would we even exist, if He had not spoken us into being?

His sacrifice on the cross for mankind is indescribable. The magnitude in which He loves us ... I just thank Him for giving me my life back.

† **Deuteronomy 28:1 (NKJV)** "Now it shall come to pass, if you diligently obey the voice of the Lord your God, to observe carefully all His commandments which I command you today, that the Lord your God will set you high above all nations of the earth

† **1 Chronicles 29:!1-13 (KJV)** "... Thine, O Lord is the greatness, and the power, and the glory, and the victory, and the majesty: for all that is in the Heaven and in the earth is thine; thine is the Kingdom, O Lord, and Thou art exalted as head above all. Both riches and honour come of thee, and thou reignest over all; and in thine hand is power and might; and in thine hand it is to make great, and to give strength unto all.

Now therefore, our God, we thank Thee, and praise thy glorious name ..."

† **Psalm 145 (KJV)** "...Thy Kingdom is an everlasting kingdom, and thy dominion endureth throughout all generations..." Our King; JESUS CHRIST & His Kingdom:

† **Isaiah 9:6-7 (KJV)** For unto us a child is born, unto us a Son is given: and the government shall be upon His shoulder: and His name shall be called Wonderful, Counsellor, The mighty God, The everlasting Father, The Prince of Peace. Of the increase of His government and peace there shall be no end, upon the throne of David, and upon His Kingdom, to order it, and to establish it with judgment and with justice from henceforth even for ever. The zeal of the Lord of hosts will perform this.

† **Isaiah 33:22 (KJV)** For the Lord is our judge, the Lord is our lawgiver, the Lord is our king; he will save us.

† **Micah 5:2-4 (MSG)** But you, Bethlehem, David's country, the runt of the litter— From you will come the leader who will shepherd-rule Israel. He'll be no upstart, no pretender. His family tree is ancient and distinguished. Meanwhile, Israel will be in foster homes until the birth pangs are over and the child is born, And the scattered brothers come back home to the family of Israel. He will stand tall in his shepherd-

rule by God's strength, centered in the majesty of God-Revealed. And the people will have a good and safe home, for the whole world will hold him in respect—Peacemaker of the world!

✝ **Matthew 11:28-30 (AMPC)** Come to Me, all you who labor and are heavy-laden and overburdened, and I will cause you to rest. [I will ease and relieve and refresh your souls.] Take My yoke upon you and learn of Me, for I am gentle (meek) and humble (lowly) in heart, and you will find rest (relief and ease and refreshment and recreation and blessed quiet) for your souls. For My yoke is wholesome (useful, good—not harsh, hard, sharp, or pressing, but comfortable, gracious, and pleasant), and My burden is light and easy to be borne.

✝ **Mark 12:35-37 (KJV)** And Jesus answered and said, while he taught in the temple, How say the scribes that Christ is the son of David? For David himself said by the Holy Ghost, The Lord said to my Lord, Sit thou on my right hand, till I make thine enemies thy footstool. David therefore himself calleth him Lord; and whence is he then his son? And the common people heard him gladly.

✝ **Luke 23:34 (AMPC)** And Jesus prayed, Father, forgive them, for they know not what they do. And they divided His garments and distributed them by casting lots for them.

† **John 1:1-3 (AMPC)** In the beginning [before all time] was the Word (Christ), and the Word was with God, and the Word was God Himself. He was present originally with God. All things were made *and* came into existence through Him; and without Him was not even one thing made that has come into being.

† **John 6:68-69 (NKJV)** But Simon Peter answered Him, "Lord, to whom shall we go? You have the words of eternal life. Also we have come to believe and know that You are the Christ, the Son of the living God."

† **John 10:10 (AMPC)** The thief comes only in order to steal and kill and destroy. I came that they may have and enjoy life, and have it in abundance (to the full, till it overflows).

† **John 10:26-28 (AMPC)** But you do not believe *and* trust *and* rely on Me because you do not belong to My fold [you are no sheep of Mine]. The sheep that are My own hear *and* are listening to My voice; and I know them, and they follow Me. And I give them eternal life, and they shall never lose it *or* perish throughout the ages. [To all eternity they shall never by any means be destroyed.] And no one is able to snatch them out of My hand.

† **John 11:25-26 (NKJV)** Jesus said to her, "I am the resurrection and the life. He who believes in Me, though he may die, he shall live. And whoever lives

and believes in Me shall never die. Do you believe this?"

† **John 14:6 (NKJV)** Jesus said to him, "I am the way, the truth, and the life. No one comes to the Father except through Me.

† **John 14:10 (KJV)** Believest thou not that I am in the Father, and the Father in me? the words that I speak unto you I speak not of myself: but the Father that dwelleth in me, he doeth the works.

† **Acts 1:2-4 (KJV)** 2. Until the day in which he was taken up, after that he through the Holy Ghost had given commandments unto the apostles whom he had chosen: 3. To whom also he shewed himself alive after his passion by many infallible proofs, being seen of them forty days, and speaking of the things pertaining to the kingdom of God: 4. And, being assembled together with them, commanded them that they should not depart from Jerusalem, but wait for the promise of the Father, which, saith he, ye have heard of me.

† **Acts 2:30 (KJV)** Therefore being a prophet, and knowing that God had sworn with an oath to him, that of the fruit of his loins, according to the flesh, he would raise up Christ to sit on his throne;

† **Romans 8:1-4 (NKJV)** There is therefore now no condemnation to those who are in Christ Jesus, who do not walk according to the flesh, but according to the Spirit. For the law of the Spirit of life in Christ Jesus

has made me free from the law of sin and death. For what the law could not do in that it was weak through the flesh, God did by sending His own Son in the likeness of sinful flesh, on account of sin: He condemned sin in the flesh, that the righteous requirement of the law might be fulfilled in us who do not walk according to the flesh but according to the Spirit.

✝ **Romans 14:7-9 (AMPC)** 7. None of us lives to himself [but to the Lord], and none of us dies to himself [but to the Lord, for] 8. If we live, we live to the Lord, and if we die, we die to the Lord. So then, whether we live or we die, we belong to the Lord. 9. For Christ died and lived again for this very purpose, that He might be Lord both of the dead and of the living.

✝ **1 Corinthians 15:23-25 (KJV)** 23. But every man in his own order: Christ the firstfruits; afterward they that are Christ's at his coming. 24. Then cometh the end, when he shall have delivered up the kingdom to God, even the Father; when he shall have put down all rule and all authority and power. 25. For he must reign, till he hath put all enemies under his feet.

✝ **2 Corinthians 3:17 (KJV)** Now the Lord is that Spirit: and where the Spirit of the Lord is, there is liberty.

✝ **Ephesians 1:19-22 (NLT)** I also pray that you will understand the incredible greatness of God's power for us who believe Him. This is the same mighty power that raised Christ from the dead and seated Him in the place of honor at God's right hand in the Heavenly realms. Now He is far above any ruler or authority or power or leader or anything else—not only in this world but also in the world to come. God has put all things under the authority of Christ and has made Him head over all things for the benefit of the church. And hath put all things under His feet, and gave Him to be the head over all things to the church, Which is His body, the fulness of Him that filleth all in all.

✝ **Philippians 2:5-11 (NKJV)** [The Humbled and Exalted Christ] Let this mind be in you which was also in Christ Jesus, who, being in the form of God, did not consider it robbery to be equal with God, but made Himself of no reputation, taking the form of a bondservant, and coming in the likeness of men. And being found in appearance as a man, He humbled Himself and became obedient to the point of death, even the death of the cross. Therefore God also has highly exalted Him and given Him the name which is above every name, that at the name of Jesus every knee should bow, of those in heaven, and of those on earth, and of those under the earth, and that every tongue should confess that Jesus Christ is Lord, to the glory of God the Father.

† **Philippians 4:9 (KJV)** Those things, which ye have both learned, and received, and heard, and seen in me, do: and the God of peace shall be with you.

† **Colossians 1:18-20 (NKJV)** And He is the head of the body, the church, who is the beginning, the firstborn from the dead, that in all things He may have the preeminence. [Reconciled in Christ] For it pleased the Father that in Him all the fullness should dwell, and by Him to reconcile all things to Himself, by Him, whether things on earth or things in heaven, having made peace through the blood of His cross.

† **1 Timothy 1:17 (KJV)** Now unto the King eternal, immortal, invisible, the only wise God, be honour and glory for ever and ever. Amen.

† **Hebrews 2:16-18 (MSG)** It's obvious, of course, that he didn't go to all this trouble for angels. It was for people like us, children of Abraham. That's why he had to enter into every detail of human life. Then, when he came before God as high priest to get rid of the people's sins, he would have already experienced it all himself—all the pain, all the testing—and would be able to help where help was needed.

† **Hebrews 2:16-18 (NKJV)** For indeed He does not give aid to angels, but He does give aid to the seed of Abraham. Therefore, in all things He had to be made like *His* brethren, that He might be a merciful and

faithful High Priest in things *pertaining* to God, to make propitiation for the sins of the people. For in that He Himself has suffered, being tempted, He is able to aid those who are tempted.

† **Hebrews 13:8 (KJV)** Jesus Christ the same yesterday, and to day, and for ever.

† **1 Peter 2:24 (KJV)** Who his own self bare our sins in his own body on the tree, that we, being dead to sins, should live unto righteousness: by whose stripes ye were healed.

† **Revelation 1:18 (NKJV)** I *am* He who lives, and was dead, and behold, I am alive forevermore. Amen. And I have the keys of Hades and of Death.

† **Revelation 1:18 (MSG)** "Don't fear: I am First, I am Last, I'm Alive. I died, but I came to life, and my life is now forever. See these keys in my hand? They open and lock Death's doors, they open and lock Hell's gates.

† **Revelation 5:12 (KJV)** Saying with a loud voice, Worthy is the Lamb that was slain to receive power, and riches, and wisdom, and strength, and honour, and glory, and blessing.

† **Revelation 19:10-17 (AMPC)** 10… Worship God! For the substance (essence) of the truth revealed by Jesus is the spirit of all prophecy [the vital breath, the

inspiration of all inspired preaching and interpretation of the divine will and purpose, including both mine and yours]. 11. After that I saw heaven opened, and behold, a white horse [appeared]! The One Who was riding it is called Faithful (Trustworthy, Loyal, Incorruptible, Steady) and True, and He passes judgment and wages war in righteousness (holiness, justice, and uprightness). 12. His eyes [blaze] like a flame of fire, and on His head are many kingly crowns (diadems); and He has a title (name) inscribed which He alone knows *or* can understand. 13. He is dressed in a robe dyed by dipping in blood, and the title by which He is called is The Word of God. 14. And the troops of heaven, clothed in fine linen, dazzling and clean, followed Him on white horses. 15. From His mouth goes forth a sharp sword with which He can smite (afflict, strike) the nations; and He will shepherd *and* control them with a staff (scepter, rod) of iron. He will tread the winepress of the fierceness of the wrath *and* indignation of God the All-Ruler (the Almighty, the Omnipotent). 16. And on His garment (robe) and on His thigh He has a name (title) inscribed, KING OF KINGS AND LORD OF LORDS. 17. Then I saw a single angel stationed in the sun's light, and with a mighty voice he shouted to all the birds that fly across the sky, Come, gather yourselves together for the great supper of God,

HOLY SPIRIT:
Our Guide & Teacher

We learn about the third Person of the Trinity; Holy Ghost in Chapters 14, 15, 16 and in Acts, but of course He is throughout the Word of God, from Genesis to Revelation. For He; Holy Spirit displays the Power of the Trinity. Thank You my Holy Spirit for dwelling with me and in me always.

- † **Genesis 1:1-2 (KJV)** In the beginning God created the heaven and the earth. And the earth was without form, and void; and darkness was upon the face of the deep. And the Spirit of God moved upon the face of the waters.

- † **Genesis 1:2 (AMPC)** The earth was without form and an empty waste, and darkness was upon the face of the very great deep. The Spirit of God was moving (hovering, brooding) over the face of the waters.

- † **John 14:17 (KJV)** Even the Spirit of truth; whom the world cannot receive, because it seeth him not, neither knoweth him: but ye know him; for he dwelleth with you, and shall be in you.

- † **John 14:26 (KJV)** But the Comforter, which is the Holy Ghost, whom the Father will send in My name,

He shall teach you all things, and bring all things to your remembrance, whatsoever I have said unto you.

† **John 16:7-10 (KJV)** Nevertheless I tell you the truth; It is expedient for you that I go away: for if I go not away, the Comforter will not come unto you; but if I depart, I will send him unto you. And when he is come, he will reprove the world of sin, and of righteousness, and of judgment: Of sin, because they believe not on me; Of righteousness, because I go to my Father, and ye see me no more;

† **John 16:13 (KJV)** Howbeit when he, the Spirit of truth, is come, he will guide you into all truth: for he shall not speak of himself; but whatsoever he shall hear, that shall he speak: and he will shew you things to come.

† **Acts 1:8 (KJV)** But ye shall receive power, after that the Holy Ghost is come upon you: and ye shall be witnesses unto me both in Jerusalem, and in all Judaea, and in Samaria, and unto the uttermost part of the earth.

† **Acts 2:2–4 (NASB)** And suddenly there came from heaven a noise like a violent rushing wind, and it filled the whole house where they were sitting. And there appeared to them tongues as of fire distributing themselves, and they rested on each one of them. And they were all filled with the Holy Spirit and began to

speak with other tongues, as the Spirit was giving them utterance.

† **Acts 2:38 (NASB)** Peter said to them, "Repent, and each of you be baptized in the name of Jesus Christ for the forgiveness of your sins; and you will receive the gift of the Holy Spirit.

† **Acts 10:38 (KJV)** How God anointed Jesus of Nazareth with the Holy Ghost and with power: who went about doing good, and healing all that were oppressed of the devil; for God was with him.

† **Romans 5:5 (KJV)** And hope maketh not ashamed; because the love of God is shed abroad in our hearts by the Holy Ghost which is given unto us.

† **Romans 8:8-11 (NKJV)** So then, those who are in the flesh cannot please God. But you are not in the flesh but in the Spirit, if indeed the Spirit of God dwells in you. Now if anyone does not have the Spirit of Christ, he is not His. And if Christ *is* in you, the body *is* dead because of sin, but the Spirit *is* life because of righteousness. But if the Spirit of Him who raised Jesus from the dead dwells in you, He who raised Christ from the dead will also give life to your mortal bodies through His Spirit who dwells in you.

† **Romans 8:14, 16 (KJV)** For as many as are led by the Spirit of God, they are the sons of God. The Spirit

itself beareth witness with our spirit, that we are the children of God:

† **Romans 8:26–27 (KJV)** Likewise the Spirit also helpeth our infirmities: for we know not what we should pray for as we ought: but the Spirit itself maketh intercession for us with groanings which cannot be uttered. And he that searcheth the hearts knoweth what is the mind of the Spirit, because he maketh intercession for the saints according to the will of God.

† **Romans 8:26 (AMPC)** So too the [Holy] Spirit comes to our aid and bears us up in our weakness; for we do not know what prayer to offer nor how to offer it worthily as we ought, but the Spirit Himself goes to meet our supplication and pleads in our behalf with unspeakable yearnings and groanings too deep for utterance.

† **Romans 14:17 (KJV)** For the kingdom of God is not meat and drink; but righteousness, and peace, and joy in the Holy Ghost.

† **1 Corinthians 2:12-14 (AMPC)** 12 Now we have not received the spirit [that belongs to] the world, but the [Holy] Spirit Who is from God, [given to us] that we might realize *and* comprehend *and* appreciate the gifts [of divine favor and blessing so freely and lavishly] bestowed on us by God. 13 And we are setting these truths forth in words not taught by human wisdom but

taught by the [Holy] Spirit, combining *and* interpreting spiritual truths with spiritual language [to those who possess the Holy Spirit]. 14 But the natural, non spiritual man does not accept *or* welcome *or* admit into his heart the gifts *and* teachings *and* revelations of the Spirit of God, for they are folly (meaningless nonsense) to him; and he is incapable of knowing them [of progressively recognizing, understanding, and becoming better acquainted with them] because they are spiritually discerned *and* estimated *and* appreciated.

† **Ephesians 6:17-19 (NKJV)** And take the helmet of salvation, and the sword of the Spirit, which is the word of God; praying always with all prayer and supplication in the Spirit, being watchful to this end with all perseverance and supplication for all the saints—and for me, that utterance may be given to me, that I may open my mouth boldly to make known the mystery of the gospel,

† **1 Thessalonians 1:5 (AMPC)** For our [preaching of the] glad tidings (the Gospel) came to you not only in word, but also in [its own inherent] power and in the Holy Spirit and with great conviction and absolute certainty [on our part]. You know what kind of men we proved [ourselves] to be among you for your good.

† **Revelation 21:9-12 (MSG)** [The City of Light] One of the Seven Angels who had carried the bowls filled with the seven final disasters spoke to me: "Come

here. I'll show you the Bride, the Wife of the Lamb." He took me away in the Spirit to an enormous, high mountain and showed me Holy Jerusalem descending out of Heaven from God, resplendent in the bright glory of God.

HOLY BIBLE:
God's Word is our How-To Manuel

The Holy Bible is our Constitution; the Word of God is our instruction manual, our guide book to go to when we need an answer to solve a problem. The Holy Bible is our book of Wisdom. *It is where we put our faith, because God said so. It may be that we don't see this Truth with our natural eyes, especially in our circumstances, Yet We Believe, that's Faith in the Word of God !!!*

God is our Creator; our Source. Who else to go to for a perfect fix. Could this be reason for so much chaos, confusion & hate in the world, because of seeking a solution from the wrong source(s)?

Yes, God gave us preachers and teachers to teach and edify us, but God still wants us to read the Bible for ourselves. We all have to learn how to rightly divide the word of truth. The Holy Bible is God talking to us. God wants some "Alone time" with each of us. Just you & Him, He wants to talk with you through His Word; His Word is very alive, because Jesus is also the Word and He is Alive (**John 1:1-2** and **Acts 1:2-3**).

† **Joshua 1:8 (KJV)** This book of the law shall not depart out of thy mouth; but thou shalt meditate therein day and night, that thou mayest observe to do according to all that is written therein: for then thou shalt make thy way prosperous, and then thou shalt have good success.

† **Proverbs 3:1-4 (NKJV)** My son, do not forget my law, But let your heart keep my commands; For length of days and long life And peace they will add to you. Let not mercy and truth forsake you; Bind them around your neck, Write them on the tablet of your heart, And so find favor and high esteem In the sight of God and man.

† **Proverbs 4:20-22 (NKJV)** My son, give attention to my words; Incline your ear to my sayings. Do not let them depart from your eyes; Keep them in the midst of your heart; For they are life to those who find them, And health to all their flesh.

† **Ecclesiastes 12:9-14 (AMPC)** 9. And furthermore, because the Preacher was wise, he [Solomon] still taught the people knowledge; and he pondered and searched out and set in order many proverbs. 10. The Preacher sought acceptable words, even to write down rightly words of truth or correct sentiment. 11. The words of the wise are like prodding goads, and firmly fixed [in the mind] like nails are the collected sayings which are given [as proceeding] from one Shepherd.

12. But about going further [than the words given by one Shepherd], my son, be warned. Of making many books there is no end [so do not believe everything you read], and much study is a weariness of the flesh. 13. All has been heard; the end of the matter is: Fear God [revere and worship Him, knowing that He is] and keep His commandments, for this is the whole of man [the full, original purpose of his creation, the object of God's providence, the root of character, the foundation of all happiness, the adjustment to all inharmonious circumstances and conditions under the sun] and the whole [duty] for every man. 14. For God shall bring every work into judgment, with every secret thing, whether it is good or evil.

† **Isaiah 40:8 (KJV)** The grass withereth, the flower fadeth: but the word of our God shall stand for ever.

† **Isaiah 55:11 (NKJV)** So shall My word be that goes forth from My mouth; It shall not return to Me void, But it shall accomplish what I please, And it shall prosper in the thing for which I sent it.

† **Matthew 8:8 (KJV)** The centurion answered and said, Lord, I am not worthy that thou shouldest come under my roof: but speak the word only, and my servant shall be healed.

† **Matthew 22:29 (KJV)** Jesus answered and said unto them, Ye do err, not knowing the scriptures, nor the power of God.

† **Luke 8:11 (KJV)** Now the parable is this: The seed is the word of God.

† **Luke 21:31-33 (KJV)** So likewise ye, when ye see these things come to pass, know ye that the kingdom of God is nigh at hand. Verily I say unto you, This generation shall not pass away, till all be fulfilled. Heaven and earth shall pass away: but my words shall not pass away.

† **John 1:1-2 (KJV)** In the beginning was the Word, and the Word was with God, and the Word was God. The same was in the beginning with God.

† **John 1:14 (KJV)** And the Word was made flesh, and dwelt among us, (and we beheld his glory, the glory as of the only begotten of the Father,) full of grace and truth.

† **John 6:63 (AMPC)** It is the Spirit Who gives life [He is the Life-giver]; the flesh conveys no benefit whatever [there is no profit in it]. The words (truths) that I have been speaking to you are spirit and life.

† **Acts 1:2-3 (AMPC)** 2. Until the day when He ascended, after He through the Holy Spirit had instructed *and* commanded the apostles (special

messengers) whom He had chosen. 3. To them also He showed Himself alive after His passion (His suffering in the garden and on the cross) by [a series of] many convincing demonstrations [unquestionable evidences and infallible proofs], appearing to them during forty days and talking [to them] about the things of the kingdom of God.

† **Hebrews 11:3 (KJV)** Through faith we understand that the worlds were framed by the word of God, so that things which are seen were not made of things which do appear.

† **Ephesians 6:17-18 (MSG)** Be prepared. You're up against far more than you can handle on your own. Take all the help you can get, every weapon God has issued, so that when it's all over but the shouting you'll still be on your feet. Truth, righteousness, peace, faith, and salvation are more than words. Learn how to apply them. You'll need them throughout your life. God's Word is an *indispensable* weapon. In the same way, prayer is essential in this ongoing warfare. Pray hard and long. Pray for your brothers and sisters. Keep your eyes open. Keep each other's spirits up so that no one falls behind or drops out.

† **2 Timothy 2:15 (KJV)** Study to shew thyself approved unto God, a workman that needeth not to be ashamed, rightly dividing the word of truth.

† **2 Timothy 3:16 (KJV)** All scripture is given by inspiration of God, and is profitable for doctrine, for reproof, for correction, for instruction in righteousness:

† **Hebrews 4:12 (KJV)** For the word of God is quick, and powerful, and sharper than any twoedged sword, piercing even to the dividing asunder of soul and spirit, and of the joints and marrow, and is a discerner of the thoughts and intents of the heart.

† **James 1:22-24 (AMPC)** But be doers of the Word [obey the message], and not merely listeners to it, betraying yourselves [into deception by reasoning contrary to the Truth]. For if anyone only listens to the Word without obeying it and being a doer of it, he is like a man who looks carefully at his [own] natural face in a mirror; For he thoughtfully observes himself, and then goes off and promptly forgets what he was like.

† **Revelation 1:1-3 (AMPC)** [This is] the revelation of Jesus Christ [His unveiling of the divine mysteries]. God gave it to Him to disclose and make known to His bond servants certain things which must shortly and speedily come to pass in their entirety. And He sent and communicated it through His angel (messenger) to His bond servant John, Who has testified to and vouched for all that he saw [in his visions], the word of God and the testimony of Jesus Christ. Blessed (happy, to be envied) is the man who reads aloud [in the

assemblies] the word of this prophecy; and blessed (happy, to be envied) are those who hear [it read] and who keep themselves true to the things which are written in it [heeding them and laying them to heart], for the time [for them to be fulfilled] is near.

† **Revelation 1:3 (MSG)** How blessed the reader! How blessed the hearers and keepers of these oracle words, all the words written in this book! Time is just about up.

CLAUDETTE GUNTER

Who WE are ?

Who we are? Just to name a few here, we are the redeemed, we are born again because we received Jesus Christ as our personal Lord and Savior, we are the righteousness of God in Christ, we are the Church; body of Christ, we are sons of God and we are the stewards over the earth.

In the beginning, we were all created by God and God Blessed us, but after Adam & Eve fall in the Garden; our spirit was no longer of God. Because of this disobedience, the Blessing that God had given us was automatically perverted into the curse. God didn't do this. Whenever we don't line up with God, we are allowing room for the devil; a "cause and effect" action. The devil perverts what God has created.

Thank God, this is why God sent His Son; Jesus to redeem us back to Himself. We now have to willingly accept Jesus as our Lord and Savior. After we accept Jesus, we need to renew our mind with the Word of God, so we can grow in faith and know what the will of God is for our lives. Even after receiving Jesus (again by our freewill--decisions), we can allow the curse effects or negative circumstances to come into our lives, when we are not following the Word of God. There is no cause for fear, nor worry, because God is always looking for us to come to Him and to change the way we were thinking and follow His ways (**Matthew 11:28-29**).

When we are out of the Will of God, we come out from under the covering of God's protection. When God is not present in our lifestyle, things lead to evil and death. Also the curse did not only come into our spirits, it affected the whole earth, atmosphere, ground, water, everything. This is the reason why bad things happen, like hurricanes and etc. We now have to bring God's light in this darkened world. I believe we can turn things around when we come into unity of the faith in Jesus. It is God's plan and He will bring it to pass by many or by few.

† **Genesis 1:26-27 (AMPC)** God said, Let Us [Father, Son, and Holy Spirit] make mankind in Our image, after Our likeness, and let them have complete authority over the fish of the sea, the birds of the air, the [tame] beasts, and over all of the earth, and over everything that creeps upon the earth. So God created man in His own image, in the image and likeness of God He created him; male and female He created them.

† **Genesis 12:2 (AMPC)** And I will make of you a great nation, and I will bless you [with abundant increase of favors] and make your name famous and distinguished, and you will be a blessing [dispensing good to others].

✝ **1 Samuel 14:6 (KJV)** …it may be that the LORD will work for us: for there is no restraint to the LORD to save by many or by few.

✝ **Psalm 1:1-3 (NKJV)** Blessed is the man Who walks not in the counsel of the ungodly, Nor stands in the path of sinners, Nor sits in the seat of the scornful; But his delight is in the law of the Lord, And in His law he meditates day and night. He shall be like a tree Planted by the rivers of water, That brings forth its fruit in its season, Whose leaf also shall not wither; And whatever he does shall prosper.

✝ **Psalm 2:8 (AMPC)** Ask of Me, and I will give You the nations as Your inheritance, and the uttermost parts of the earth as Your possession.

✝ **Psalm 105:15 (NKJV)** Saying, "Do not touch My anointed ones, And do My prophets no harm."

✝ **Psalm 115:16 (KJV)** The heaven, even the heavens, are the Lord's: but the earth hath he given to the children of men.

✝ **Proverbs 20:27 (KJV)** The spirit of man is the candle of the Lord, searching all the inward parts of the belly.

✝ **Proverbs 28:1 (KJV)** The wicked flee when no man pursueth: but the righteous are bold as a lion.

† **Ecclesiastes 10:5-7 (NKJV)** There is an evil I have seen under the sun, As an error proceeding from the ruler: Folly is set in great dignity, While the rich sit in a lowly place. I have seen servants on horses, While princes walk on the ground like servants.

† **Ecclesiastes 8:4 (NKJV)** Where the word of a king *is, there is* power;

† **Matthew 5:9 (KJV)** Blessed are the peacemakers: for they shall be called the children of God.

† **Matthew 5:13-16 (KJV)** Ye are the salt of the earth: but if the salt have lost his savour, wherewith shall it be salted? it is thenceforth good for nothing, but to be cast out, and to be trodden under foot of men. Ye are the light of the world. A city that is set on an hill cannot be hid. Neither do men light a candle, and put it under a bushel, but on a candlestick; and it giveth light unto all that are in the house. Let your light so shine before men, that they may see your good works, and glorify your Father which is in heaven.

† **Matthew 7:20-23 (AMPC)** Therefore, you will fully know them by their fruits. Not everyone who says to Me, Lord, Lord, will enter the kingdom of heaven, but he who does the will of My Father Who is in heaven. Many will say to Me on that day, Lord, Lord, have we not prophesied in Your name and driven out demons in Your name and done many mighty works in Your

name? And then I will say to them openly (publicly), I never knew you; depart from Me, you who act wickedly [disregarding My commands].

† **Matthew 11:28-30 (MSG)** "Are you tired? Worn out? Burned out on religion? Come to me. Get away with me and you'll recover your life. I'll show you how to take a real rest. Walk with me and work with me—watch how I do it. Learn the unforced rhythms of grace. I won't lay anything heavy or ill-fitting on you. Keep company with me and you'll learn to live freely and lightly."

† **Matthew 11:28-29 (NKJV)** Come to Me, all *you* who labor and are heavy laden, and I will give you rest. Take My yoke upon you and learn from Me, for I am gentle and lowly in heart, and you will find rest for your souls.

† **Matthew 16:16-19 (KJV)** And Simon Peter answered and said, Thou art the Christ, the Son of the living God. And Jesus answered and said unto him, Blessed art thou, Simon Barjona: for flesh and blood hath not revealed it unto thee, but my Father which is in heaven. And I say also unto thee, That thou art Peter, and upon this rock I will build my church; and the gates of hell shall not prevail against it. And I will give unto thee the keys of the kingdom of heaven: and whatsoever thou shalt bind on earth shall be bound in

heaven: and whatsoever thou shalt loose on earth shall be loosed in heaven.

† **<u>Luke 17:21 (KJV)</u>** Neither shall they say, Lo here! or, lo there! for, behold, the kingdom of God is within you.

† **<u>Luke 18:7-8 (AMPC)</u>** And will not [our just] God defend *and* protect *and* avenge His elect (His chosen ones), who cry to Him day and night? Will He defer them *and* delay help on their behalf? I tell you, He will defend *and* protect *and* avenge them speedily. However, when the Son of Man comes, will He find [persistence in] faith on the earth?

† **<u>John 13:34-35 (NKJV)</u>** A new commandment I give to you, that you love one another; as I have loved you, that you also love one another. By this all will know that you are My disciples, if you have love for one another."

† **<u>John 15:15 (NKJV)</u>** No longer do I call you servants, for a servant does not know what his master is doing; but I have called you friends, for all things that I heard from My Father I have made known to you.

† **<u>John 15:16 (NKJV)</u>** You did not choose Me, but I chose you and appointed you that you should go and bear fruit, and that your fruit should remain, that whatever you ask the Father in My name He may give you.

† **John 15:18-19 (KJV)** If the world hate you, ye know that it hated me before it hated you. If ye were of the world, the world would love his own: but because ye are not of the world, but I have chosen you out of the world, therefore the world hateth you.

† **Acts 2:4 (KJV)** And they were all filled with the Holy Ghost, and began to speak with other tongues, as the Spirit gave them utterance.

† **Romans 5:18-19 (AMPC)** Well then, as one man's trespass [one man's false step and falling away led] to condemnation for all men, so one Man's act of righteousness [leads] to acquittal and right standing with God and life for all men. For just as by one man's disobedience (failing to hear, heedlessness, and carelessness) the many were constituted sinners, so by one Man's obedience the many will be constituted righteous (made acceptable to God, brought into right standing with Him).

† **Romans 8:14 (KJV)** For as many as are led by the Spirit of God, they are the sons of God.

† **Romans 8:17 (KJV)** And if children, then heirs; heirs of God, and joint-heirs with Christ; if so be that we suffer with him, that we may be also glorified together.

† **Romans 8:19 (KJV)** "For the earnest expectation of the creature waiteth for the manifestation of the sons of God."

† **Romans 10:9-10 (KJV)** That if thou shalt confess with thy mouth the Lord Jesus, and shalt believe in thine heart that God hath raised him from the dead, thou shalt be saved. For with the heart man believeth unto righteousness; and with the mouth confession is made unto salvation.

† **Romans 12:1 (KJV)** "I beseech you therefore, brethren, by the mercies of God, that ye present your bodies a living sacrifice, holy, acceptable unto God, which is your reasonable service."

† **1 Corinthians 2:16 (KJV)** For who hath known the mind of the Lord, that he may instruct him? but we have the mind of Christ.

† **1 Corinthians 6:19-20 (KJV)** What? know ye not that your body is the temple of the Holy Ghost which is in you, which ye have of God, and ye are not your own? For ye are bought with a price: therefore glorify God in your body, and in your spirit, which are God's.

† **1 Corinthians 12:12 (NLT)** "The human body has many parts, but the many parts make up one whole body. So it is with the body of Christ."

† **2 Corinthians 5:17 (KJV)** Therefore if any man be in Christ, he is a new creature: old things are passed away; behold, all things are become new.

† **2 Corinthians 5:19-21 (AMPC)** It was God [personally present] in Christ, reconciling and restoring the world to favor with Himself, not counting up and holding against [men] their trespasses [but cancelling them], and committing to us the message of reconciliation (of the restoration to favor). So we are Christ's ambassadors, God making His appeal as it were through us. We [as Christ's personal representatives] beg you for His sake to lay hold of the divine favor [now offered you] and be reconciled to God. For our sake He made Christ [virtually] to be sin Who knew no sin, so that in and through Him we might become [endued with, viewed as being in, and examples of] the righteousness of God [what we ought to be, approved and acceptable and in right relationship with Him, by His goodness].

† **Galatians 3:13-14 (KJV)** Christ hath redeemed us from the curse of the law, being made a curse for us: for it is written, Cursed is every one that hangeth on a tree: That the blessing of Abraham might come on the Gentiles through Jesus Christ; that we might receive the promise of the Spirit through faith.

† **Galatians 3:29 (AMPC)** And if you belong to Christ [are in Him Who is Abraham's Seed], then you are

Abraham's offspring and [spiritual] heirs according to promise.

† **Ephesians 1:11-14 (NKJV)** In Him also we have obtained an inheritance, being predestined according to the purpose of Him who works all things according to the counsel of His will, that we who first trusted in Christ should be to the praise of His glory. In Him you also trusted, after you heard the word of truth, the gospel of your salvation; in whom also, having believed, you were sealed with the Holy Spirit of promise, who is the guarantee of our inheritance until the redemption of the purchased possession, to the praise of His glory.

† **Ephesians 1:19-23 (KJV)** And what is the exceeding greatness of his power to us-ward who believe, according to the working of his mighty power, Which he wrought in Christ, when he raised him from the dead, and set him at his own right hand in the heavenly places, Far above all principality, and power, and might, and dominion, and every name that is named, not only in this world, but also in that which is to come: And hath put all things under his feet, and gave him to be the head over all things to the church, Which is his body, the fulness of him that filleth all in all.

† **Ephesians 2:8 (KJV)** For by grace are ye saved through faith; and that not of yourselves: it is the gift of God:

† **Ephesians 2:10 (KJV)** For we are his workmanship, created in Christ Jesus unto good works, which God hath before ordained that we should walk in them.

† **Ephesians 3:8-12 (AMPC)** To me, though I am the very least of all the saints (God's consecrated people), this grace (favor, privilege) was granted and graciously entrusted: to proclaim to the Gentiles the unending (boundless, fathomless, incalculable, and exhaustless) riches of Christ [wealth which no human being could have searched out], Also to enlighten all men and make plain to them what is the plan [regarding the Gentiles and providing for the salvation of all men] of the mystery kept hidden through the ages and concealed until now in [the mind of] God Who created all things by Christ Jesus [The purpose is] that through the church the complicated, many-sided wisdom of God in all its infinite variety and innumerable aspects might now be made known to the angelic rulers and authorities (principalities and powers) in the heavenly sphere. This is in accordance with the terms of the eternal and timeless purpose which He has realized and carried into effect in [the person of] Christ Jesus our Lord, In Whom, because of our faith in Him, we dare to have the boldness (courage and confidence) of free access (an unreserved approach to God with freedom and without fear).

† **Ephesians 3:9-11 (KJV)** And to make all men see what is the fellowship of the mystery, which from the beginning of the world hath been hid in God, who created all things by Jesus Christ: To the intent that now unto the principalities and powers in heavenly places might be known by the church the manifold wisdom of God, According to the eternal purpose which he purposed in Christ Jesus our Lord:

† **Ephesians 4:22-24 (KJV)** That ye put off concerning the former conversation the old man, which is corrupt according to the deceitful lusts; And be renewed in the spirit of your mind; And that ye put on the new man, which after God is created in righteousness and true holiness.

† **Ephesians 4:22-24 (AMPC)** Strip yourselves of your former nature [put off and discard your old unrenewed self] which characterized your previous manner of life and becomes corrupt through lusts and desires that spring from delusion; And be constantly renewed in the spirit of your mind [having a fresh mental and spiritual attitude], And put on the new nature (the regenerate self) created in God's image, [Godlike] in true righteousness and holiness.

† **Philippians 2:5 (KJV)** Let this mind be in you, which was also in Christ Jesus:

† **Colossians 1:25-27 (KJV)** Whereof I am made a minister, according to the dispensation of God which is given to me for you, to fulfil the word of God; Even the mystery which hath been hid from ages and from generations, but now is made manifest to his saints: To whom God would make known what is the riches of the glory of this mystery among the Gentiles; which is Christ in you, the hope of glory:

† **1 Thessalonians 5:23 (KJV)** And the very God of peace sanctify you wholly; and I pray God your whole spirit and soul and body be preserved blameless unto the coming of our Lord Jesus Christ.

† **1 Peter 1:17-19 (AMPC)** And if you call upon Him as [your] Father Who judges each one impartially according to what he does, [then] you should conduct yourselves with true reverence throughout the time of your temporary residence [on the earth, whether long or short]. You must know (recognize) that you were redeemed (ransomed) from the useless (fruitless) way of living inherited by tradition from [your] forefathers, not with corruptible things [such as] silver and gold. But [you were purchased] with the precious blood of Christ (the Messiah), like that of a [sacrificial] lamb without blemish or spot.

† **1 Peter 1:23 (AMPC)** You have been regenerated (born again), not from a mortal origin (seed, sperm),

but from one that is immortal by the ever living and lasting Word of God.

✝ **1 Peter 2:9 (KJV)** But ye are a chosen generation, a royal priesthood, an holy nation, a peculiar people; that ye should shew forth the praises of him who hath called you out of darkness into his marvellous light;

✝ **1 John 4:4 (KJV)** Ye are of God, little children, and have overcome them: because greater is he that is in you, than he that is in the world.

✝ **1 John 4:6 (KJV)** We are of God: he that knoweth God heareth us; he that is not of God heareth not us. Hereby know we the spirit of truth, and the spirit of error.

✝ **Revelation 5:9-10 (AMPC)** And [now] they sing a new song, saying, You are worthy to take the scroll and to break the seals that are on it, for You were slain (sacrificed), and with Your blood You purchased men unto God from every tribe and language and people and nation. And You have made them a kingdom (royal race) and priests to our God, and they shall reign [as kings] over the earth!

Why are WE here ?

These are just a few of the many promises of God and the gifts He has given to us, when we are born again. Just like anything, for example: a toddler learning how to walk, likewise we have to learn the things of God. We have to renew our mind with the Word of God to obtain the things that are freely given to us by God. When we don't renew our minds, we can't recognize these precious promises/benefits. We can't hear the voice of the Lord in order to be led by the Holy Spirit. All of this was made available, because of what Jesus did for us on the cross. We can't make anything happen in our own strength with lasting value. We need God !!!

This means, we will live way beneath the royal status that we have in Jesus, if we don't do things God's way. We are here to live as kings on this earth, for we are sons of God; heir of God and joint heirs with Christ.

To get anything from God, we have to speak it; we have to say something (prayer, confessing, decreeing). God made us a speaking spirit, like Him. This is why the words that we speak are so important, because these words are spirit and they are (living) life. We have what we SAY, remember that! If we don't want a certain thing to happen, don't speak it. Our spirit helps us bring things to pass, in our actions, after it is spoken, so let's not confuse our spirit.

Be focused. Faith comes by hearing and hearing by the Word of God. Say what God says, for we are never a liar, when we say what He says about us; who we are, what we are to do and have. When we are in agreement with what God says, so be it, Expect it !!!

We are here to continue to do God's will. God's plan for man, before the fall of Adam and Eve in the Garden of Eden was to spread that Beautiful Garden, which was full of Love and provision all over the earth.

Now, we have another opportunity to do God's will. God sent His son into the world, born of an earthly woman, so that He (God) can do His work through a willing vessel (human) in the earth. Because God gave us the freewill to make our own decisions. We can decide to live and thrive in God or listen to the lies of the enemy; satan and be sick and defeated all our lives and die young. All of this is by the testimony of our mouth, what we are saying is how our lives will play out.

Are we confessing life or death? We are here in the world to stop the suffering and injustices. Jesus has already defeated the enemy, but we have to walk it out in our lives. God has to have a man or woman or even a child to ask for His help (**2 Chronicles 7:14**), which is allowing Him to come in their lives through prayer and using His Word in the Bible. When we speak and meditate on His Word, Holy Spirit will bring His will to pass (**Isaiah 55:11**), through us as His willing vessels.

† **Genesis 1:28 (AMPC)** And God blessed them and said to them, Be fruitful, multiply, and fill the earth, and subdue it [using all its vast resources in the service of God and man]; and have dominion over the fish of the sea, the birds of the air, and over every living creature that moves upon the earth.

† **Genesis 11:1-7 (KJV)** 1. And the whole earth was of one language, and of one speech. 2. And it came to pass, as they journeyed from the east, that they found a plain in the land of Shinar; and they dwelt there. 3. And they said one to another, Go to, let us make brick, and burn them thoroughly. And they had brick for stone, and slime had they for morter. 4. And they said, Go to, let us build us a city and a tower, whose top may reach unto heaven; and let us make us a name, lest we be scattered abroad upon the face of the whole earth. 5. And the Lord came down to see the city and the tower, which the children of men builded. 6. And the Lord said, Behold, the people is one, and they have all one language; and this they begin to do: and now nothing will be restrained from them, which they have imagined to do. 7. Go to, let us go down, and there confound their language, that they may not understand one another's speech.

† **Genesis 14:18-23 (NKJV)** [Abram and Melchizedek] 18. Then Melchizedek king of Salem brought out bread and wine; he *was* the priest of God Most High.

19. And he blessed him and said: "Blessed be Abram of God Most High, Possessor of heaven and earth; 20. And blessed be God Most High, Who has delivered your enemies into your hand." And he gave him a tithe of all. 21. Now the king of Sodom said to Abram, "Give me the persons, and take the goods for yourself." 22. But Abram said to the king of Sodom, "I have raised my hand to the Lord, God Most High, the Possessor of heaven and earth, 23. That I *will take* nothing, from a thread to a sandal strap, and that I will not take anything that *is* yours, lest you should say, 'I have made Abram rich'—

† **Numbers 6:24-26 (KJV)** The LORD bless thee, and keep thee: The LORD make his face shine upon thee, and be gracious unto thee: The LORD lift up his countenance upon thee, and give thee peace.

† **Deuteronomy 6:11 (KJV)** And houses full of all good things, which thou filledst not, and wells digged, which thou diggedst not, vineyards and olive trees, which thou plantedst not; when thou shalt have eaten and be full;

† **Deuteronomy 15:1-3 (MSG)** At the end of every seventh year, cancel all debts. This is the procedure: Everyone who has lent money to a neighbor writes it off. You must not press your neighbor or his brother for payment: All-Debts-Are Canceled—God says so. You may collect payment from foreigners, but

whatever you have lent to your fellow Israelite you must write off.

† **Deuteronomy 28:13 (KJV)** And the LORD shall make thee the head, and not the tail; and thou shalt be above only, and thou shalt not be beneath; if that thou hearken unto the commandments of the LORD thy God, which I command thee this day, to observe and to do them:

† **Deuteronomy 30:19 (KJV)** I call heaven and earth to record this day against you, that I have set before you life and death, blessing and cursing: therefore choose life, that both thou and thy seed may live:

† **Deuteronomy 31:6 (NKJV)** Be strong and of good courage, do not fear nor be afraid of them; for the Lord your God, He is the One who goes with you. He will not leave you nor forsake you."

† **1 Samuel 17:29 (KJV)** And David said, What have I now done? Is there not a cause?

† **1 Samuel 17:45-47 (KJV)** Then said David to the Philistine, Thou comest to me with a sword, and with a spear, and with a shield: but I come to thee in the name of the Lord of hosts, the God of the armies of Israel, whom thou hast defied. This day will the Lord deliver thee into mine hand; and I will smite thee, and take thine head from thee; and I will give the carcases of the host of the Philistines this day unto the fowls of the

air, and to the wild beasts of the earth; that all the earth may know that there is a God in Israel. And all this assembly shall know that the Lord saveth not with sword and spear: for the battle is the Lord's, and he will give you into our Hands.

† **1 Samuel 30:8 (KJV)** And David enquired at the Lord, saying, Shall I pursue after this troop? shall I overtake them? And he answered him, Pursue: for thou shalt surely overtake them, and without fail recover all.

† **2 Kings 4:1-6 (KJV)** 1. Now there cried a certain woman of the wives of the sons of the prophets unto Elisha, saying, Thy servant my husband is dead; and thou knowest that thy servant did fear the Lord: and the creditor is come to take unto him my two sons to be bondmen. 2. And Elisha said unto her, What shall I do for thee? tell me, what hast thou in the house? And she said, Thine handmaid hath not any thing in the house, save a pot of oil. 3. Then he said, Go, borrow thee vessels abroad of all thy neighbours, even empty vessels; borrow not a few. 4. And when thou art come in, thou shalt shut the door upon thee and upon thy sons, and shalt pour out into all those vessels, and thou shalt set aside that which is full. 5. So she went from him, and shut the door upon her and upon her sons, who brought the vessels to her; and she poured out. 6. And it came to pass, when the vessels were full, that she said unto her son, Bring me yet a vessel. And he

said unto her, There is not a vessel more. And the oil stayed.

† **2 Chronicles 7:14 (KJV)** If my people, which are called by my name, shall humble themselves, and pray, and seek my face, and turn from their wicked ways; then will I hear from heaven, and will forgive their sin, and will heal their land.

† **2 Chronicles 15:2-4 (NKJV)** And he went out to meet Asa, and said to him: "Hear me, Asa, and all Judah and Benjamin. The LORD *is* with you while you are with Him. If you seek Him, He will be found by you; but if you forsake Him, He will forsake you. For a long time Israel *has been* without the true God, without a teaching priest, and without law; but when in their trouble they turned to the LORD God of Israel, and sought Him, He was found by them.

† **2 Chronicles 20:20 (KJV)** And they rose early in the morning, and went forth into the wilderness of Tekoa: and as they went forth, Jehoshaphat stood and said, Hear me, O Judah, and ye inhabitants of Jerusalem; Believe in the Lord your God, so shall ye be established; believe his prophets, so shall ye prosper.

† **Nehemiah 8:10 (KJV)** Then he said unto them, Go your way, eat the fat, and drink the sweet, and send portions unto them for whom nothing is prepared: for

this day is holy unto our Lord: neither be ye sorry; for the joy of the Lord is your strength.

† **Job 22:28 (KJV)** Thou shalt also decree a thing, and it shall be established unto thee: and the light shall shine upon thy ways.

† **Job 36:11 (NKJV)** If they obey and serve *Him,* They shall spend their days in prosperity, And their years in pleasures.

† **Psalm 19:14 (KJV)** Let the words of my mouth, and the meditation of my heart, be acceptable in thy sight, O Lord, my strength, and my redeemer.

† **Psalm 23:1-6 (KJV)** The Lord is my shepherd; I shall not want. He maketh me to lie down in green pastures: he leadeth me beside the still waters. He restoreth my soul: he leadeth me in the paths of righteousness for his name's sake. Yea, though I walk through the valley of the shadow of death, I will fear no evil: for thou art with me; thy rod and thy staff they comfort me. Thou preparest a table before me in the presence of mine enemies: thou anointest my head with oil; my cup runneth over. Surely goodness and mercy shall follow me all the days of my life: and I will dwell in the house of the Lord for ever.

† **Psalm 27:13-14 (AMPC)** [What, what would have become of me] had I not believed that I would see the

Lord's goodness in the land of the living! Wait *and* hope for *and* expect the Lord; be brave *and* of good courage and let your heart be stout *and* enduring. Yes, wait for *and* hope for *and* expect the Lord.

† **Psalm 35:27 (KJV)** Let them shout for joy, and be glad, that favour my righteous cause: yea, let them say continually, Let the Lord be magnified, which hath pleasure in the prosperity of his servant.

† **Psalm 41:1-2 (AMPC)** Blessed (happy, fortunate, to be envied) is he who considers the weak and the poor; the Lord will deliver him in the time of evil and trouble. The Lord will protect him and keep him alive; he shall be called blessed in the land; and You will not deliver him to the will of his enemies.

† **Psalm 75:6-7 (KJV)** For promotion cometh neither from the east, nor from the west, nor from the south. But God is the judge: he putteth down one, and setteth up another.

† **Psalm 82 (NKJV)** "God stands in the congregation of the mighty; He judges among the gods. How long will you judge unjustly, And show partiality to the wicked? Selah Defend the poor and fatherless; Do justice to the afflicted and needy. Deliver the poor and needy; Free them from the hand of the wicked. They do not know, nor do they understand; They walk about in darkness; All the foundations of the earth are unstable.

I said, "You are gods, And all of you are children of the Most High. But you shall die like men, And fall like one of the princes." Arise, O god, judge the earth; For you shall inherit all nations.

† **Psalm 91:1-16 (KJV)** He that dwelleth in the secret place of the most High shall abide under the shadow of the Almighty. I will say of the Lord, He is my refuge and my fortress: my God; in him will I trust...

† **Psalm 91:11-12 (KJV)** For he shall give his angels charge over thee, to keep thee in all thy ways. They shall bear thee up in their hands, lest thou dash thy foot against a stone.

† **Psalm 91 (KJV)** 1. He that dwelleth in the secret place of the most High shall abide under the shadow of the Almighty. 2. I will say of the Lord, He is my refuge and my fortress: my God; in him will I trust. 3. Surely he shall deliver thee from the snare of the fowler, and from the noisome pestilence. 4. He shall cover thee with his feathers, and under his wings shalt thou trust: his truth shall be thy shield and buckler. 5. Thou shalt not be afraid for the terror by night; nor for the arrow that flieth by day; 6. Nor for the pestilence that walketh in darkness; nor for the destruction that wasteth at noonday. 7. A thousand shall fall at thy side, and ten thousand at thy right hand; but it shall not come nigh thee. 8. Only with thine eyes shalt thou behold and see the reward of the wicked. 9. Because

thou hast made the Lord, which is my refuge, even the most High, thy habitation; 10. There shall no evil befall thee, neither shall any plague come nigh thy dwelling. 11. For he shall give his angels charge over thee, to keep thee in all thy ways. 12. They shall bear thee up in their hands, lest thou dash thy foot against a stone. 13. Thou shalt tread upon the lion and adder: the young lion and the dragon shalt thou trample under feet. 14. Because he hath set his love upon me, therefore will I deliver him: I will set him on high, because he hath known my name. 15. He shall call upon me, and I will answer him: I will be with him in trouble; I will deliver him, and honour him. 16. With long life will I satisfy him, and shew him my salvation.

✝ **Psalm 100 (KJV)** 1. Make a joyful noise unto the Lord, all ye lands. 2. Serve the Lord with gladness: come before his presence with singing. 3. Know ye that the Lord he is God: it is he that hath made us, and not we ourselves; we are his people, and the sheep of his pasture. 4. Enter into his gates with thanksgiving, and into his courts with praise: be thankful unto him, and bless his name. 5. For the Lord is good; his mercy is everlasting; and his truth endureth to all generations.

✝ **Psalm 103:1-22 (KJV)** 1. Bless the Lord, O my soul: and all that is within me, bless his holy name. 2. Bless the Lord, O my soul, and forget not all his benefits: 3. Who forgiveth all thine iniquities; who healeth all thy diseases; 4. Who redeemeth thy life from destruction;

who crowneth thee with lovingkindness and tender mercies; 5. Who satisfieth thy mouth with good things; so that thy youth is renewed like the eagle's. 6. The Lord executeth righteousness and judgment for all that are oppressed. 7. He made known his ways unto Moses, his acts unto the children of Israel. 8. The Lord is merciful and gracious, slow to anger, and plenteous in mercy. 9. He will not always chide: neither will he keep his anger for ever. 10. He hath not dealt with us after our sins; nor rewarded us according to our iniquities. 11. For as the heaven is high above the earth, so great is his mercy toward them that fear him. 12. As far as the east is from the west, so far hath he removed our transgressions from us. 13. Like as a father pitieth his children, so the Lord pitieth them that fear him. 14. For he knoweth our frame; he remembereth that we are dust. 15. As for man, his days are as grass: as a flower of the field, so he flourisheth. 16. For the wind passeth over it, and it is gone; and the place thereof shall know it no more. 17. But the mercy of the Lord is from everlasting to everlasting upon them that fear him, and his righteousness unto children's children; 18. To such as keep his covenant, and to those that remember his commandments to do them. 19. The Lord hath prepared his throne in the heavens; and his kingdom ruleth over all. 20. Bless the Lord, ye his angels, that excel in strength, that do his commandments, hearkening unto the voice of his word. 21. Bless ye the Lord, all ye his hosts; ye ministers of his, that do his pleasure. 22. Bless the

Lord, all his works in all places of his dominion: bless the Lord, O my soul.

† **Psalm 111:10 (KJV)** The fear of the Lord is the beginning of wisdom: a good understanding have all they that do his commandments: his praise endureth for ever.

† **Psalm 115:16 (KJV)** The heaven, even the heavens, are the Lord's: but the earth hath he given to the children of men.

† **Psalm 118:17 (KJV)** I shall not die, but live, and declare the works of the Lord.

† **Psalm 138:7-8 (NKJV)** Though I walk in the midst of trouble, You will revive me; You will stretch out Your hand Against the wrath of my enemies, And Your right hand will save me. The LORD will perfect *that which* concerns me; Your mercy, O LORD, *endures* forever; Do not forsake the works of Your hands.

† **Psalm 150 (KJV).** 1.Praise ye the LORD. Praise God in his sanctuary: praise him in the firmament of his power. 2. Praise him for his mighty acts: praise him according to his excellent greatness. 3. Praise him with the sound of the trumpet: praise him with the psaltery and harp. 4. Praise him with the timbrel and dance: praise him with stringed instruments and organs. 5. Praise him upon the loud cymbals: praise him upon the

high sounding cymbals. 6. Let every thing that hath breath praise the LORD. Praise ye the LORD.

✝ **Isaiah 55:11 (NKJV)** So shall My word be that goes forth from My mouth; It shall not return to Me void, But it shall accomplish what I please, And it shall prosper *in the thing* for which I sent it.

✝ **Proverbs 3:5-6 (KJV)** Trust in the Lord with all thine heart; and lean not unto thine own understanding. In all thy ways acknowledge him, and he shall direct thy paths.

✝ **Proverbs 3:7-8 (KJV)** Be not wise in thine own eyes: fear the Lord, and depart from evil. It shall be health to thy navel, and marrow to thy bones.

✝ **Proverbs 3:9 (KJV)** Honour the Lord with thy substance, and with the firstfruits of all thine increase:

✝ **Proverbs 4:7 (KJV)** Wisdom is the principal thing; therefore get wisdom: and with all thy getting get understanding.

✝ **Proverbs 4:23 (KJV)** Keep thy heart with all diligence; for out of it are the issues of life.

✝ **Proverbs 10:22 (NIV)** The blessing of the Lord brings wealth, without painful toil for it.

† **Proverbs 18:21 (KJV)** Death and life are in the power of the tongue: and they that love it shall eat the fruit thereof.

† **Proverbs 19:17 (AMPC)** He who has pity on the poor lends to the Lord, and that which he has given He will repay to him.

† **Isaiah 26:3 (KJV)** Thou wilt keep him in perfect peace, whose mind is stayed on thee: because he trusteth in thee.

† **Isaiah 40:31 (KJV)** But they that wait upon the Lord shall renew their strength; they shall mount up with wings as eagles; they shall run, and not be weary; and they shall walk, and not faint.

† **Isaiah 41:10 (NKJV)** Fear not, for I *am* with you; Be not dismayed, for I *am* your God. I will strengthen you, Yes, I will help you, I will uphold you with My righteous right hand.'

† **Isaiah 48:17 (KJV)** Thus saith the Lord, thy Redeemer, the Holy One of Israel; I am the Lord thy God which teacheth thee to profit, which leadeth thee by the way that thou shouldest go.

† **Isaiah 51:3-4 (NKJV)** For the Lord will comfort Zion, He will comfort all her waste places; He will make her wilderness like Eden, And her desert like the garden of the Lord; Joy and gladness will be found in it,

Thanksgiving and the voice of melody. "Listen to Me, My people; And give ear to Me, O My nation: For law will proceed from Me, And I will make My justice rest As a light of the peoples.

✝ **Isaiah 51:16 (KJV)** And I have put my words in thy mouth, and I have covered thee in the shadow of mine hand, that I may plant the heavens, and lay the foundations of the earth, and say unto Zion, Thou art my people.

✝ **Isaiah 53:4-5 (NKJV)** Surely He has borne our griefs And carried our sorrows; Yet we esteemed Him stricken, Smitten by God, and afflicted. But He was wounded for our transgressions, He was bruised for our iniquities; The chastisement for our peace was upon Him, And by His stripes we are healed.

✝ **Isaiah 54:17 (NKJV)** No weapon formed against you shall prosper, And every tongue which rises against you in judgment You shall condemn. This is the heritage of the servants of the Lord, And their righteousness is from Me," Says the Lord.

✝ **Isaiah 55:1-3 (AMPC)** Wait and listen, everyone who is thirsty! Come to the waters; and he who has no money, come, buy and eat! Yes, come, buy [priceless, spiritual] wine and milk without money and without price [simply for the self-surrender that accepts the blessing]. Why do you spend your money for that which is not bread, and your earnings for what does not satisfy? Hearken diligently to Me, and eat what is good, and let your soul delight itself in fatness [the profuseness of spiritual joy]. Incline your ear [submit and consent to the divine will] and come to Me; hear, and your soul will revive; and I will make an everlasting covenant or league with you, even the sure mercy (kindness, goodwill, and compassion) promised to David.

† **Isaiah 55:10-11 (AMPC)** For as the rain and snow come down from the heavens, and return not there again, but water the earth and make it bring forth and sprout, that it may give seed to the sower and bread to the eater, So shall My word be that goes forth out of My mouth: it shall not return to Me void [without producing any effect, useless], but it shal accomplish that which I please *and* purpose, and it shall prosper in the thing for which I sent it.

† **Isaiah 58:6-7 (KJV)** Is not this the fast that I have chosen? to loose the bands of wickedness, to undo the heavy burdens, and to let the oppressed go free, and that ye break every yoke? Is it not to deal thy bread to the hungry, and that thou bring the poor that are cast out to thy house? when thou seest the naked, that thou cover him; and that thou hide not thyself from thine own flesh?

† **Isaiah 58:11-12 (NKJV)** The Lord will guide you continually, And satisfy your soul in drought, And

strengthen your bones; You shall be like a watered garden, And like a spring of water, whose waters do not fail. Those from among you Shall build the old waste places; You shall raise up the foundations of many generations; And you shall be called the Repairer of the Breach, The Restorer of Streets to Dwell In.

† **Isaiah 61:1-4 (KJV)** 1. The Spirit of the Lord God is upon me; because the Lord hath anointed me to preach good tidings unto the meek; he hath sent me to bind up the brokenhearted, to proclaim liberty to the captives, and the opening of the prison to them that are bound; 2. To proclaim the acceptable year of the Lord, and the day of vengeance of our God; to comfort all that mourn; 3. To appoint unto them that mourn in Zion, to give unto them beauty for ashes, the oil of joy for mourning, the garment of praise for the spirit of heaviness; that they might be called trees of righteousness, the planting of the Lord, that he might be glorified. 4. And they shall build the old wastes, they shall raise up the former desolations, and they shall repair the waste cities, the desolations of many generations.

† **Ezekiel 36:27 (KJV)** And I will put my spirit within you, and cause you to walk in my statutes, and ye shall keep my judgments, and do them.

† **Daniel 11:32 (KJV)** And such as do wickedly against the covenant shall he corrupt by flatteries: but the people that do know their God shall be strong, and do exploits.

† **Hosea 4:6 (KJV)** My people are destroyed for lack of knowledge: because thou hast rejected knowledge, I will also reject thee, that thou shalt be no priest to me: seeing thou hast forgotten the law of thy God, I will also forget thy children.

† **Joel 2:25 (KJV)** And I will restore to you the years that the locust hath eaten, the cankerworm, and the caterpiller, and the palmerworm, my great army which I sent among you.

† **Joel 2:28 (KJV)** And it shall come to pass afterward, that I will pour out my spirit upon all flesh; and your sons and your daughters shall prophesy, your old men shall dream dreams, your young men shall see visions:

† **Habakkuk 2:2-3 (KJV)** And the Lord answered me, and said, Write the vision, and make it plain upon tables, that he may run that readeth it. For the vision is yet for an appointed time, but at the end it shall speak, and not lie: though it tarry, wait for it; because it will surely come, it will not tarry.

† **Malachi 3:10 (KJV)** Bring ye all the tithes into the storehouse, that there may be meat in mine house, and prove me now herewith, saith the Lord of hosts, if I

will not open you the windows of heaven, and pour you out a blessing, that there shall not be room enough to receive it.

† **Matthew 5:16 (KJV)** Let your light so shine before men, that they may see your good works, and glorify your Father which is in heaven.

† **Matthew 6:20-21 (KJV)** But lay up for yourselves treasures in heaven, where neither moth nor rust doth corrupt, and where thieves do not break through nor steal: For where your treasure is, there will your heart be also.

† **Matthew 6:33 (AMPC)** But seek (aim at and strive after) first of all His kingdom and His righteousness (His way of doing and being right), and then all these things taken together will be given you besides.

† **Matthew 8:8 (KJV)** The centurion answered and said, Lord, I am not worthy that thou shouldest come under my roof: but speak the word only, and my servant shall be healed.

† **Matthew 16:19 (CEV)** I will give you the keys to the kingdom of heaven, and God in heaven will allow whatever you allow on earth. But he will not allow anything that you don't allow.

† **Matthew 16:19 (NKJV)** And I will give you the keys of the kingdom of heaven, and whatever you bind on

earth will be bound in heaven, and whatever you loose on earth will be loosed in heaven."

† **Matthew 18:19-20 (KJV)** Again I say unto you, That if two of you shall agree on earth as touching any thing that they shall ask, it shall be done for them of My Father which is in heaven. For where two or three are gathered together in My name, there am I in the midst of them.

† **Matthew 28:18-20 (KJV)** And Jesus came and spake unto them, saying, All power is given unto me in heaven and in earth. Go ye therefore, and teach all nations, baptizing them in the name of the Father, and of the Son, and of the Holy Ghost: Teaching them to observe all things whatsoever I have commanded you: and, lo, I am with you always, even unto the end of the world. Amen.

† **Mark 5:36 (KJV)** As soon as Jesus heard the word that was spoken, ... Be not afraid, only believe.

† **Mark 11:22-25 (KJV)** And Jesus answering saith unto them, Have faith in God. For verily I say unto you, That whosoever shall say unto this mountain, Be thou removed, and be thou cast into the sea; and shall not doubt in his heart, but shall believe that those things which he saith shall come to pass; he shall have whatsoever he saith. Therefore I say unto you, What things soever ye desire, when ye pray, believe that ye

receive them, and ye shall have them. And when ye stand praying, forgive, if ye have ought against any: that your Father also which is in heaven may forgive you your trespasses.

✝ **Mark 16:17-18 (KJV)** And these signs shall follow them that believe; In My name shall they cast out devils; they shall speak with new tongues; They shall take up serpents; and if they drink any deadly thing, it shall not hurt them; they shall lay hands on the sick, and they shall recover.

✝ **Luke 6:27-28 (NKJV)** [Love Your Enemies] "But I say to you who hear: Love your enemies, do good to those who hate you, bless those who curse you, and pray for those who spitefully use you.

✝ **Luke 6:38 (NKJV)** Give, and it will be given to you: good measure, pressed down, shaken together, and running over will be put into your bosom. For with the same measure that you use, it will be measured back to you."

✝ **Luke 6:45 (KJV)** A good man out of the good treasure of his heart bringeth forth that which is good; and an evil man out of the evil treasure of his heart bringeth forth that which is evil: for of the abundance of the heart his mouth speaketh.

† **Luke 18:8 (KJV)** I tell you that he will avenge them speedily. Nevertheless when the Son of man cometh, shall he find faith on the earth?

† **Luke 19:13 (KJV)** And he called his ten servants, and delivered them ten pounds, and said unto them, Occupy till I come.

† **John 2:1-5 (NASB)** [Miracle at Cana] On the third day there was a wedding in Cana of Galilee, and the mother of Jesus was there; and both Jesus and His disciples were invited to the wedding. When the wine ran out, the mother of Jesus *said to Him, "They have no wine." And Jesus *said to her, "Woman, what does that have to do with us? My hour has not yet come." His mother *said to the servants, "Whatever He says to you, do it."

† **John 3:16 (KJV)** For God so loved the world, that he gave his only begotten Son, that whosoever believeth in him should not perish, but have everlasting life.

† **John 3:15-19 (AMPC)** In order that everyone who believes in Him [who cleaves to Him, trusts Him, and relies on Him] may *not perish, but* have eternal life *and* [actually] live forever! For God so greatly loved *and* dearly prized the world that He [even] gave up His only begotten (unique) Son, so that whoever believes in (trusts in, clings to, relies on) Him shall not perish (come to destruction, be lost) but have eternal (everlasting) life. For God did not send the Son into

the world in order to judge (to reject, to condemn, to pass sentence on) the world, but that the world might find salvation *and* be made safe *and* sound through Him. He who believes in Him [who clings to, trusts in, relies on Him] is not judged [he who trusts in Him never comes up for judgment; for him there is no rejection, no condemnation—he incurs no damnation]; but he who does not believe (cleave to, rely on, trust in Him) is judged already [he has already been convicted and has already received his sentence] because he has not believed in *and* trusted in the name of the only begotten Son of God. [He is condemned for refusing to let his trust rest in Christ's name.] The [basis of the] judgment (indictment, the test by which men are judged, the ground for the sentence) lies in this: the Light has come into the world, and people have loved the darkness rather than *and* more than the Light, for their works (deeds) were evil.

† **John 6:63 (KJV)** It is the spirit that quickeneth; the flesh profiteth nothing: the words that I speak unto you, they are spirit, and they are life.

† **John 8:31-32 (NKJV)** Then Jesus said to those Jews who believed Him, "If you abide in My word, you are My disciples indeed. And you shall know the truth, and the truth shall make you free."

† **John 14:12 (KJV)** Verily, verily, I say unto you, He that believeth on me, the works that I do shall he do

also; and greater works than these shall he do; because I go unto my Father.

† **Acts 2:1-3 (KJV)** And when the day of Pentecost was fully come, they were all with one accord in one place. And suddenly there came a sound from heaven as of a rushing mighty wind, and it filled all the house where they were sitting. And there appeared unto them cloven tongues like as of fire, and it sat upon each of them.

† **Acts 2:44-47 (AMPC)** And all who believed (who adhered to and trusted in and relied on Jesus Christ) were united and [together] they had everything in common; And they sold their possessions (both their landed property and their movable goods) and distributed the price among all, according as any had need. And day after day they regularly assembled in the temple with united purpose, and in their homes they broke bread [including the Lord's Supper]. They partook of their food with gladness and simplicity and generous hearts, Constantly praising God and being in favor and goodwill with all the people; and the Lord kept adding [to their number] daily those who were being saved [from spiritual death].

† **Romans 1:16-17 (KJV)** For I am not ashamed of the gospel of Christ: for it is the power of God unto salvation to every one that believeth; to the Jew first, and also to the Greek. For therein is the righteousness

of God revealed from faith to faith: as it is written, The just shall live by faith.

† **Romans 3:4 (KJV)** God forbid: yea, let God be true, but every man a liar; as it is written, That thou mightest be justified in thy sayings, and mightest overcome when thou art judged.

† **Romans 4:17 (KJV)** (As it is written, I have made thee a father of many nations,) before him whom he believed, even God, who quickeneth the dead, and calleth those things which be not as though they were.

† **Romans 8:1 (KJV)** There is therefore now no condemnation to them which are in Christ Jesus, who walk not after the flesh, but after the Spirit.

† **Romans 8:5-7 (AMPC)** For those who are according to the flesh and are controlled by its unholy desires set their minds on and pursue those things which gratify the flesh, but those who are according to the Spirit and are controlled by the desires of the Spirit set their minds on and seek those things which gratify the [Holy] Spirit. Now the mind of the flesh [which is sense and reason without the Holy Spirit] is death [death that comprises all the miseries arising from sin, both here and hereafter]. But the mind of the [Holy] Spirit is life and [soul] peace [both now and forever]. [That is] because the mind of the flesh [with its carnal

thoughts and purposes] is hostile to God, for it does not submit itself to God's Law; indeed it cannot.

† **Romans 8:11 (KJV)** But if the Spirit of him that raised up Jesus from the dead dwell in you, he that raised up Christ from the dead shall also quicken your mortal bodies by his Spirit that dwelleth in you.

† **Romans 8:19 (AMPC)** For [even the whole] creation (all nature) waits expectantly *and* longs earnestly for God's sons to be made known [waits for the revealing, the disclosing of their sonship].

† **Romans 8:30-32 (KJV)** 30. Moreover whom he did predestinate, them he also called: and whom he called, them he also justified: and whom he justified, them he also glorified. 31. What shall we then say to these things? If God be for us, who can be against us? 32. He that spared not his own Son, but delivered him up for us all, how shall he not with him also freely give us all things?

† **Romans 8:37 (KJV)** Nay, in all these things we are more than conquerors through him that loved us.

† **Romans 10:17 (NKJV)** So then faith comes by hearing, and hearing by the word of God.

† **Romans 12:2 (KJV)** And be not conformed to this world: but be ye transformed by the renewing of your mind, that ye may prove what is that good, and acceptable, and perfect, will of God.

† **Romans 12:3-8 (KJV)** 3. For I say, through the grace given unto me, to every man that is among you, not to think of himself more highly than he ought to think; but to think soberly, according as God hath dealt to every man the measure of faith. 4. For as we have many members in one body, and all members have not the same office: 5. So we, being many, are one body in Christ, and every one members one of another. 6. Having then gifts differing according to the grace that is given to us, whether prophecy, let us prophesy according to the proportion of faith; 7. Or ministry, let us wait on our ministering: or he that teacheth, on teaching; 8. Or he that exhorteth, on exhortation: he that giveth, let him do it with simplicity; he that ruleth, with diligence; he that sheweth mercy, with cheerfulness.

† **Romans 12:19 (KJV)** Dearly beloved, avenge not yourselves, but rather give place unto wrath: for it is written, Vengeance is mine; I will repay, saith the Lord.

† **Romans 13:8 (KJV)** Owe no man any thing, but to love one another: for he that loveth another hath fulfilled the law.

† **Romans 13:8 (AMPC)** Keep out of debt and owe no man anything, except to love one another; for he who loves his neighbor [who practices loving others] has

fulfilled the Law [relating to one's fellowmen, meeting all its requirements].

† **Romans 14:19 (AMPC)** So let us then definitely aim for *and* eagerly pursue what makes for harmony and for mutual upbuilding (edification and development) of one another.

† **2 Corinthians 1:20-22 (NKJV)** For all the promises of God in Him *are* Yes, and in Him Amen, to the glory of God through us. Now He who establishes us with you in Christ and has anointed us *is* God, Who also has sealed us and given us the Spirit in our hearts as a guarantee.

† **1 Corinthians 1:26-31 (MSG)** Take a good look, friends, at who you were when you got called into this life. I don't see many of "the brightest and the best" among you, not many influential, not many from high-society families. Isn't it obvious that God deliberately chose men and women that the culture overlooks and exploits and abuses, chose these "nobodies" to expose the hollow pretensions of the "somebodies"? That makes it quite clear that none of you can get by with blowing your own horn before God. Everything that we have—right thinking and right living, a clean slate and a fresh start—comes from God by way of Jesus Christ. That's why we have the saying, "If you're going to blow a horn, blow a trumpet for God."

† **1 Corinthians 1:26-31 (NKJV)** [Glory Only in the Lord] 26. For you see your calling, brethren, that not many wise according to the flesh, not many mighty, not many noble, *are called.* 27. But God has chosen the foolish things of the world to put to shame the wise, and God has chosen the weak things of the world to put to shame the things which are mighty; 28. and the base things of the world and the things which are despised God has chosen, and the things which are not, to bring to nothing the things that are, 29. that no flesh should glory in His presence. 30. But of Him you are in Christ Jesus, who became for us wisdom from God—and righteousness and sanctification and redemption—31. that, as it is written, "He who glories, let him glory in the Lord."

† **1 Corinthians 1:30 (KJV)** But of him are ye in Christ Jesus, who of God is made unto us wisdom, and righteousness, and sanctification, and redemption:

† **1 Corinthians 2:11-13 (NKJV)** For what man knows the things of a man except the spirit of the man which is in him? Even so no one knows the things of God except the Spirit of God. Now we have received, not the spirit of the world, but the Spirit who is from God, that we might know the things that have been freely given to us by God. These things we also speak, not in words which man's wisdom teaches but which the Holy Spirit teaches, comparing spiritual things with spiritual.

† **1 Corinthians 2:16 (KJV)** For who hath known the mind of the Lord, that he may instruct him? but we have the mind of Christ.

† **1 Corinthians 10:13 (KJV)** There hath no temptation taken you but such as is common to man: but God is faithful, who will not suffer you to be tempted above that ye are able; but will with the temptation also make a way to escape, that ye may be able to bear it.

† **1 Corinthians 11:23-26 (NKJV)** [Institution of the Lord's Supper] For I received from the Lord that which I also delivered to you: that the Lord Jesus on the same night in which He was betrayed took bread; and when He had given thanks, He broke it and said, "Take, eat; this is My body which is broken for you; do this in remembrance of Me." In the same manner He also took the cup after supper, saying, "This cup is the new covenant in My blood. This do, as often as you drink it, in remembrance of Me." For as often as you eat this bread and drink this cup, you proclaim the Lord's death till He comes.

† **1 Corinthians 12:1-11 (AMPC)** 1. Now about the spiritual gifts (the special endowments of supernatural energy), brethren, I do not want you to be misinformed. 2. You know that when you were heathen, you were led off after idols that could not speak [habitually] as impulse directed and whenever

the occasion might arise. 3. Therefore I want you to understand that no one speaking under the power and influence of the [Holy] Spirit of God can [ever] say, Jesus be cursed! And no one can [really] say, Jesus is [my] Lord, except by and under the power and influence of the Holy Spirit. 4. Now there are distinctive varieties and distributions of endowments (gifts, extraordinary powers distinguishing certain Christians, due to the power of divine grace operating in their souls by the Holy Spirit) and they vary, but the [Holy] Spirit remains the same. 5. And there are distinctive varieties of service and ministration, but it is the same Lord [Who is served]. 6. And there are distinctive varieties of operation [of working to accomplish things], but it is the same God Who inspires and energizes them all in all. 7. But to each one is given the manifestation of the [Holy] Spirit [the evidence, the spiritual illumination of the Spirit] for good and profit. 8. To one is given in and through the [Holy] Spirit [the power to speak] a message of wisdom, and to another [the power to express] a word of knowledge and understanding according to the same [Holy] Spirit; 9. To another [wonder-working] faith by the same [Holy] Spirit, to another the extraordinary powers of healing by the one Spirit; 10. To another the working of miracles, to another prophetic insight (the gift of interpreting the divine will and purpose); to another the ability to discern and distinguish between [the utterances of true] spirits [and false ones], to another various kinds of [unknown] tongues, to another the ability to interpret [such] tongues. 11. All these [gifts, achievements, abilities] are inspired and brought to pass by one and the same [Holy] Spirit, Who apportions to each person individually [exactly] as He chooses.

† **1 Corinthians 12:12-13 (KJV)** For as the body is one, and hath many members, and all the members of that one body, being many, are one body: so also is Christ. For by one Spirit are we all baptized into one body, whether we be Jews or Gentiles, whether we be bond or free; and have been all made to drink into one Spirit.

† **1 Corinthians 12:14-21 (AMPC)** 14. For the body does not consist of one limb or organ but of many. 15. If the foot should say, Because I am not the hand, I do not belong to the body, would it be therefore not [a part] of the body? 16. If the ear should say, Because I am not the eye, I do not belong to the body, would it be therefore not [a part] of the body? 17. If the whole body were an eye, where [would be the sense of] hearing? If the whole body were an ear, where [would be the sense of] smell? 18. But as it is, God has placed and arranged the limbs and organs in the body, each [particular one] of them, just as He wished and saw fit and with the best adaptation. 19. But if [the whole] were all a single organ, where would the body be? 20. And now there are [certainly] many limbs and organs, but a single body. 21. And the eye is not able to say to

the hand, I have no need of you, nor again the head to the feet, I have no need of you.

† **1 Corinthians 12:27-28 (AMPC)** Now you [collectively] are Christ's body and [individually] you are members of it, each part severally and distinct [each with his own place and function]. So God has appointed some in the church [for His own use]: first apostles (special messengers); second prophets (inspired preachers and expounders); third teachers; then wonder-workers; then those with ability to heal the sick; helpers; administrators; [speakers in] different (unknown) tongues.

† **1 Corinthians 15:57 (KJV)** But thanks be to God, which giveth us the victory through our Lord Jesus Christ.

† **2 Corinthians 2:14 (KJV)** Now thanks be unto God, which always causeth us to triumph in Christ, and maketh manifest the savour of his knowledge by us in every place.

† **2 Corinthians 5:7 (KJV)** (For we walk by faith, not by sight:)

† **2 Corinthians 5:17-19 (NKJV)** Therefore, if anyone *is* in Christ, *he is* a new creation; old things have passed away; behold, all things have become new. Now all things *are* of God, who has reconciled us to

Himself through Jesus Christ, and has given us the ministry of reconciliation, that is, that God was in Christ reconciling the world to Himself, not imputing their trespasses to them, and has committed to us the word of reconciliation.

† **2 Corinthians 8:9 (NKJV)** For you know the grace of our Lord Jesus Christ, that though He was rich, yet for your sakes He became poor, that you through His poverty might become rich.

† **2 Corinthians 8:9 (AMPC)** For you are becoming progressively acquainted with *and* recognizing more strongly *and* clearly the grace of our Lord Jesus Christ (His kindness, His gracious generosity, His undeserved favor and spiritual blessing), [in] that though He was [so very] rich, yet for your sakes He became [so very] poor, in order that by His poverty you might become enriched (abundantly supplied).

† **2 Corinthians 9:8 (AMPC)** And God is able to make all grace (every favor and earthly blessing) come to you in abundance, so that you may always and under all circumstances and whatever the need be self-sufficient [possessing enough to require no aid or support and furnished in abundance for every good work and charitable donation].

† **2 Corinthians 10:4-5** (For the weapons of our warfare are not carnal, but mighty through God to the pulling down of strong holds;) Casting down imaginations,

and every high thing that exalteth itself against the knowledge of God, and bringing into captivity every thought to the obedience of Christ.

† **2 Corinthians 12:9 (KJV)** And he said unto me, My grace is sufficient for thee: for my strength is made perfect in weakness. Most gladly therefore will I rather glory in my infirmities, that the power of Christ may rest upon me.

† **Galatians 2:20 (KJV)** I am crucified with Christ: nevertheless I live; yet not I, but Christ liveth in me: and the life which I now live in the flesh I live by the faith of the Son of God, who loved me, and gave himself for me.

† **Galatians 5:21-23 (KJV)** Envyings, murders, drunkenness, revellings, and such like: of the which I tell you before, as I have also told you in time past, that they which do such things shall not inherit the kingdom of God. But the fruit of the Spirit is love, joy, peace, longsuffering, gentleness, goodness, faith, Meekness, temperance: against such there is no law.

† **Galatians 5:22-23 (AMPC)** But the fruit of the [Holy] Spirit [the work which His presence within accomplishes] is love, joy (gladness), peace, patience (an even temper, forbearance), kindness, goodness (benevolence), faithfulness, Gentleness (meekness, humility), self-control (self-restraint, continence).

Against such things there is no law [that can bring a charge].

† **Ephesians 1:17 (KJV)** That the God of our Lord Jesus Christ, the Father of glory, may give unto you the spirit of wisdom and revelation in the knowledge of him:

† **Ephesians 4:12-16 (KJV)** For the perfecting of the saints, for the work of the ministry, for the edifying of the body of Christ: Till we all come in the unity of the faith, and of the knowledge of the Son of God, unto a perfect man, unto the measure of the stature of the fulness of Christ: That we henceforth be no more children, tossed to and fro, and carried about with every wind of doctrine, by the sleight of men, and cunning craftiness, whereby they lie in wait to deceive; But speaking the truth in love, may grow up into him in all things, which is the head, even Christ: From whom the whole body fitly joined together and compacted by that which every joint supplieth, according to the effectual working in the measure of every part, maketh increase of the body unto the edifying of itself in love.

† **Ephesians 5:1 (AMPC)** Therefore be imitators of God [copy Him and follow His example], as well-beloved children [imitate their father].

† **Ephesians 5:8-10 (KJV)** For ye were sometimes darkness, but now are ye light in the Lord: walk as children of light: (For the fruit of the Spirit is in all goodness and righteousness and truth;) Proving what is acceptable unto the Lord.

† **Ephesians 6:10-11 (KJV)** Finally, my brethren, be strong in the Lord, and in the power of his might. Put on the whole armour of God, that ye may be able to stand against the wiles of the devil.

† **Ephesians 6:10-11 (AMPC)** In conclusion, be strong in the Lord [be empowered through your union with Him]; draw your strength from Him [that strength which His boundless might provides]. Put on God's whole armor [the armor of a heavy-armed soldier which God supplies], that you may be able successfully to stand up against [all] the strategies and the deceits of the devil.

† **Ephesians 6:16 (KJV)** Above all, taking the shield of faith, wherewith ye shall be able to quench all the fiery darts of the wicked.

† **Ephesians 6:16 (AMPC)** Lift up over all the [covering] shield of saving faith, upon which you can quench all the flaming missiles of the wicked [one].

† **Philippians 2:1-4 (NKJV)** [Unity Through Humility] Therefore if there is any consolation in Christ, if any

comfort of love, if any fellowship of the Spirit, if any affection and mercy, fulfill my joy by being like-minded, having the same love, being of one accord, of one mind. Let nothing be done through selfish ambition or conceit, but in lowliness of mind let each esteem others better than himself. Let each of you look out not only for his own interests, but also for the interests of others.

† **Philippians 2:12-16 (NKJV)** [Light Bearers] Therefore, my beloved, as you have always obeyed, not as in my presence only, but now much more in my absence, work out your own salvation with fear and trembling; for it is God who works in you both to will and to do for His good pleasure. Do all things without complaining and disputing, that you may become blameless and harmless, children of God without fault in the midst of a crooked and perverse generation, among whom you shine as lights in the world, holding fast the word of life, so that I may rejoice in the day of Christ that I have not run in vain or labored in vain.

† **Philippians 4:6 (AMPC)** Do not fret *or* have any anxiety about anything, but in every circumstance *and* in everything, by prayer and petition (definite requests), with thanksgiving, continue to make your wants known to God.

† **Philippians 4:6-8 (KJV)** Be careful for nothing; but in every thing by prayer and supplication with

thanksgiving let your requests be made known unto God. And the peace of God, which passeth all understanding, shall keep your hearts and minds through Christ Jesus.Finally, brethren, whatsoever things are true, whatsoever things are honest, whatsoever things are just, whatsoever things are pure, whatsoever things are lovely, whatsoever things are of good report; if there be any virtue, and if there be any praise, think on these things.

† **Philippians 4:8 (NLT)** And now, dear brothers and sisters, one final thing. Fix your thoughts on what is true, and honorable, and right, and pure, and lovely, and admirable. Think about things that are excellent and worthy of praise.

† **Philippians 4:13 (KJV)** I can do all things through Christ which strengtheneth me.

† **Philippians 4:15 (AMPC)** And you Philippians yourselves well know that in the early days of the Gospel ministry, when I left Macedonia, no church (assembly) entered into partnership with me and opened up [a debit and credit] account in giving and receiving except you only.

† **Colossians 3:15-17 (KJV)** And let the peace of God rule in your hearts, to the which also ye are called in one body; and be ye thankful. Let the word of Christ dwell in you richly in all wisdom; teaching and

admonishing one another in psalms and hymns and spiritual songs, singing with grace in your hearts to the Lord. And whatsoever ye do in word or deed, do all in the name of the Lord Jesus, giving thanks to God and the Father by him.

† **1 Thessalonians 1:2-4 (KJV)** We give thanks to God always for you all, making mention of you in our prayers; Remembering without ceasing your work of faith, and labour of love, and patience of hope in our Lord Jesus Christ, in the sight of God and our Father; Knowing, brethren beloved, your election of God.

† **1 Thessalonians 5:8-10 (NKJV)** But let us who are of the day be sober, putting on the breastplate of faith and love, and as a helmet the hope of salvation. For God did not appoint us to wrath, but to obtain salvation through our Lord Jesus Christ, who died for us, that whether we wake or sleep, we should live together with Him.

† **1 Thessalonians 5:23 (KJV)** And the very God of peace sanctify you wholly; and I pray God your whole spirit and soul and body be preserved blameless unto the coming of our Lord Jesus Christ.

† **1 Timothy 2:1-6 (KJV)** I exhort therefore, that, first of all, supplications, prayers, intercessions, and giving of thanks, be made for all men; For kings, and for all that are in authority; that we may lead a quiet and

peaceable life in all godliness and honesty. For this is good and acceptable in the sight of God our Saviour; Who will have all men to be saved, and to come unto the knowledge of the truth. For there is one God, and one mediator between God and men, the man Christ Jesus; Who gave himself a ransom for all, to be testified in due time.

† **2 Timothy 1:7 (KJV)** For God hath not given us the spirit of fear; but of power, and of love, and of a sound mind.

† **Hebrews 1:14 (AMPC)** Are not the angels all ministering spirits (servants) sent out in the service [of God for the assistance] of those who are to inherit salvation?

† **Hebrews 7:1-2 (KJV)** For this Melchisedec, king of Salem, priest of the most high God, who met Abraham returning from the slaughter of the kings, and blessed him; To whom also Abraham gave a tenth part of all; first being by interpretation King of righteousness, and after that also King of Salem, which is, King of peace;

† **Hebrews 10:30 (KJV)** For we know him that hath said, Vengeance belongeth unto me, I will recompense, saith the Lord. And again, The Lord shall judge his people.

† **Hebrews 10:35 (KJV)** Cast not away therefore your confidence, which hath great recompence of reward.

† **Hebrews 11:1 (KJV)** Now faith is the substance of things hoped for, the evidence of things not seen.

† **Hebrews 11:1-3 (MSG)** The fundamental fact of existence is that this trust in God, this faith, is the firm foundation under everything that makes life worth living. It's our handle on what we can't see. The act of faith is what distinguished our ancestors, set them above the crowd. By faith, we see the world called into existence by God's word, what we see created by what we don't see.

† **Hebrews 11:2-3 (KJV)** For by it the elders obtained a good report. Through faith we understand that the worlds were framed by the word of God, so that things which are seen were not made of things which do appear.

† **Hebrews 11:6 (KJV)** But without faith it is impossible to please him: for he that cometh to God must believe that he is, and that he is a rewarder of them that diligently seek him.

† **Hebrews 13:5 (KJV)** Let your conversation be without covetousness; and be content with such things as ye have: for he hath said, I will never leave thee, nor forsake thee.

† **Hebrews 13:5 (AMPC)** Let your character *or* moral disposition be free from love of money [including greed, avarice, lust, and craving for earthly possessions] and be satisfied with your present [circumstances and with what you have]; for He [God] Himself has said, I will not in any way fail you *nor* give you up *nor* leave you without support. [I will] not, [I will] not, [I will] not in any degree leave you helpless *nor* forsake *nor* let [you] down (relax My hold on you)! [Assuredly not!]

† **James 1:5 (KJV)** If any of you lack wisdom, let him ask of God, that giveth to all men liberally, and upbraideth not; and it shall be given him.

† **James 1:16-18 (AMPC)** 16. Do not be misled, my beloved brethren. 17. Every good gift and every perfect (free, large, full) gift is from above; it comes down from the Father of all [that gives] light, in [the shining of] Whom there can be no variation [rising or setting] or shadow cast by His turning [as in an eclipse]. 18. And it was of His own [free] will that He gave us birth [as sons] by [His] Word of Truth, so that we should be a kind of firstfruits of His creatures [a sample of what He created to be consecrated to Himself].

† **James 4:7 (KJV)** Submit yourselves therefore to God. Resist the devil, and he will flee from you.

✝ **James 5:16 (KJV)** The effectual fervent prayer of a righteous man availeth much.

✝ **1 Peter 1:2 (AMPC)** Who were chosen and foreknown by God the Father and consecrated (sanctified, made holy) by the Spirit to be obedient to Jesus Christ (the Messiah) and to be sprinkled with [His] blood: May grace (spiritual blessing) and peace be given you in increasing abundance [that spiritual peace to be realized in and through Christ, freedom from fears, agitating passions, and moral conflicts].

✝ **1 Peter 4:10-11 (KJV)** As every man hath received the gift, even so minister the same one to another, as good stewards of the manifold grace of God. If any man speak, let him speak as the oracles of God; if any man minister, let him do it as of the ability which God giveth: that God in all things may be glorified through Jesus Christ, to whom be praise and dominion for ever and ever. Amen.

✝ **1 Peter 5:7 (AMPC)** Casting the whole of your care [all your anxieties, all your worries, all your concerns, once and for all] on Him, for He cares for you affectionately and cares about you watchfully.

✝ **2 Peter 1:3-11 (KJV)** 3. According as his divine power hath given unto us all things that pertain unto life and godliness, through the knowledge of him that hath called us to glory and virtue: 4. Whereby are given unto us exceeding great and precious promises: that by these ye might be partakers of the divine nature, having escaped the corruption that is in the world through lust. 5. And beside this, giving all diligence, add to your faith virtue; and to virtue knowledge; 6. And to knowledge temperance; and to temperance patience; and to patience godliness; 7. And to godliness brotherly kindness; and to brotherly kindness charity. 8. For if these things be in you, and abound, they make you that ye shall neither be barren nor unfruitful in the knowledge of our Lord Jesus Christ. 9. But he that lacketh these things is blind, and cannot see afar off, and hath forgotten that he was purged from his old sins. 10. Wherefore the rather, brethren, give diligence to make your calling and election sure: for if ye do these things, ye shall never fall: 11. For so an entrance shall be ministered unto you abundantly into the everlasting kingdom of our Lord and Saviour Jesus Christ.

† **1 John 1:7 (KJV)** But if we walk in the light, as He is in the light, we have fellowship one with another, and the blood of Jesus Christ His Son cleanseth us from all sin.

† **1 John 2:20 (KJV)** But ye have an unction from the Holy One, and ye know all things.

† **1 John 2:27 (KJV)** But the anointing which ye have received of him abideth in you, and ye need not that

any man teach you: but as the same anointing teacheth you of all things, and is truth, and is no lie, and even as it hath taught you, ye shall abide in him.

† **1 John 3:1-2 (KJV)** Behold, what manner of love the Father hath bestowed upon us, that we should be called the sons of God: therefore the world knoweth us not, because it knew him not. Beloved, now are we the sons of God, and it doth not yet appear what we shall be: but we know that, when he shall appear, we shall be like him; for we shall see him as he is.

† **1 John 3:23-24 (NKJV)** And this is His commandment: that we should believe on the name of His Son Jesus Christ and love one another, as He gave us commandment. Now he who keeps His commandments abides in Him, and He in him. And by this we know that He abides in us, by the Spirit whom He has given us.

† **1 John 4:17 (KJV)** Herein is our love made perfect, that we may have boldness in the day of judgment: because as he is, so are we in this world.

† **3 John 2 (KJV)** Beloved, I wish above all things that thou mayest prosper and be in health, even as thy soul prospereth.

† **Revelation 1:5-6 (KJV)** And from Jesus Christ, who is the faithful witness, and the first begotten of the

dead, and the prince of the kings of the earth. Unto him that loved us, and washed us from our sins in his own blood, And hath made us kings and priests unto God and his Father; to him be glory and dominion for ever and ever. Amen.

† **<u>Revelation 12:11 (KJV)</u>** And they overcame him by the blood of the Lamb, and by the word of their testimony; and they loved not their lives unto the death.

ABOUT THE AUTHOR

Author Central on Amazon
https://www.amazon.com/Claudette-Gunter/e/B072N2HRVH

Other Book(s)

GIVING IS GOD: A PRACTICAL GUIDE TO GIVING
Both Amazon Paperback & Kindle e-book
https://www.amazon.com/dp/B07219R7KJ

Barnes and Noble Hardcover
https://www.barnesandnoble.com/w/giving-is-god-claudette-gunter/1126623504?ean=9780999083307

MIND, WHAT ARE YOU THINKING?
Both Amazon Paperback & Kindle e-book
https://www.amazon.com/dp/B073PP263G

CONNECT WITH US

https://www.kingdomofGodflag.com/

https://www.facebook.com/ClaudetteGunterBiz

http://www.twitter.com/IAcknowledgeHim

http://www.linkedin.com/in/Claudette-Gunter

www.ingramcontent.com/pod-product-compliance
Lightning Source LLC
Chambersburg PA
CBHW022115090426
42743CB00008B/861